Woke Fragility
(a parody!)

Bringing Moderates to Heel

D1313452

The Tired Moderate

Author's Note

"Woe to him inside a nonconformist clique who does not conform with nonconformity."
— *Eric Hoffer*

This book is unapologetically rooted in identity politics. I am Woke and addressing a common phenomenon - the impure, yet salvageable moderate. Though the impure moderate is this book's subject, I will be speaking directly to other Woke, as they are the only demographic that will not immediately dismiss me as full of crap.

The unWoke moderate is, unknowingly, stuck. Meandering about on the path to enlightenment, they require our guidance. We must help the unWoke reach racial nirvana[1]. This may jar the unWoke, many of whom go about their daily lives trying to pay bills, raise their kids, maintain some semblance of a social life, and, in 2020, deal with Covid-19, all while doing their best to treat those around them with dignity and respect, regardless of race.

Many moderates argue they are not racist simply because they have met some arbitrary benchmarks such as:

- Not believing skin color implies any manner of superiority or inferiority.
- Years of genuinely affable workplace relationships, including hiring, reporting to, and mentoring people of color, all without a single complaint.
- Voting for non-white politicians.
- Having many non-white friends.
- Looking up to non-white people as role models.
- Marrying someone outside their race.
- Admitting White Privilege exists and offering to help.
- Adopting a child outside of their race (Web search: "ibram kendi adoption")

---

1 I sincerely apologize to all Hindus, Buddhists, Jainists, and any other non-white people I may have offended by appropriating the word "nirvana." Trust that I struggled immensely with the decision, and have reached what I hope is a meaningful balance by using it, and pledging to confess what I've done to the next person of Indian descent I happen across.

- Claiming to not know what the hell you are talking about and just wanting to finish putting their groceries in the car in peace.

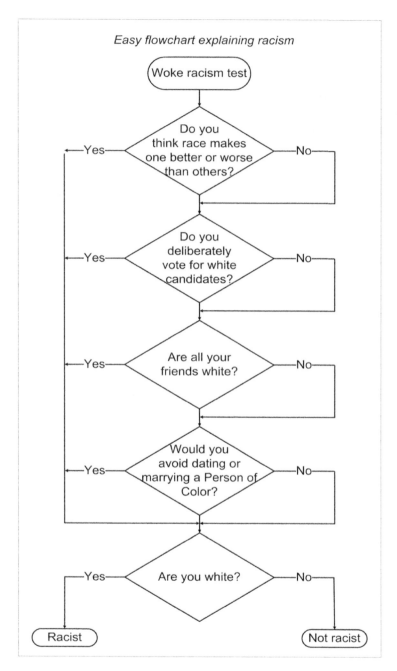

An alternate test may be performed if you have physical access to the subject and a hand mirror. Simply hold the mirror in front of their nose. If it fogs up and they are white, they are racist.

These superficial gestures mask the simple truth that there is no bar high enough. There is and will never be a test capable of proving the unWoke liberal isn't a simmering pot of racist dreck, trapped in a feedback loop of their own making that torments them with their sinful inadequacies regardless of how many non-white strangers they hug, how many subconsciously racist conversations they disrupt at dinner parties, or how many books they write. They will NEVER BE GOOD ENOUGH, just like their mothers told them from the time they could walk, until, after earning a Master's Degree, they knocked sheepishly on their childhood door, wishing - begging - for simple acknowledgment, but knowing that maternal love was a dream meant for everyone else but them.

Being unWoke is a transitional stage on the path to enlightenment. When I say "We" or "Us", I mean the Woke - the moral, the virtuous, the transcendent. I have foregone traditional citations in favor of tagging points with search terms the reader may use for further reading. Not because I prefer lazily moralizing to actual scholarship, but because requiring data to back up assertions is an oppressive tool of the white patriarchy, and properly citing my work would set a racist precedent.

Also, I've limited the scope of this book to America. I tried to "go global," but every time I explained to recent immigrants that America was a uniquely racist country they laughed at me. Further investigation uncovered data that indicated America is actually quite tolerant compared to the rest of the world, painting a picture of a very imperfect country filled with overwhelmed and anxious, but good, people, struggling to come to terms with the clear racism they are already ashamed of in their national history, while acknowledging they live amazingly well by global standards.

I have chosen to exclude these data.

Table of Contents

Introduction

"There's a time to think, and a time to act. And this, gentlemen, is no time to think."
— *Sheriff Bud Boomer*

White people are racist.

No matter how soothing my tone of voice is when I tell them this, they invariably get upset. unWoke liberals are the worst. It's almost like they've grown up believing that racism is only slightly less repugnant than pedophilia, and I'm now linking them directly to it in front of their coworkers. I should mention that I do this sort of thing in public. In fact, I make a living by traveling from company to company, holding lectures on race relations[2].

Many people have predictably negative reactions to learning from someone who knows nothing about them that they are racist. Some have gone decades getting along with people of all ethnicities, so you can imagine their surprise! In fact, singling out a group of people as morally inferior based on their skin color, while they sit with people they have to work and get along with long after I leave, uncovers many dormant, racist attitudes that manifest themselves in emotional displays quite unbecoming.

Some people become angry and defensive, stating that they treat everybody equally. This overlooks the benefits they unwittingly receive by virtue of their "whiteness," a term most have never heard before. One inevitably asks why I'm castigating an entire group of people for something they didn't ask for and can't change, especially when they agree that data indicate systemic racism does in fact exist in areas such as prison

---

2   I'm lying, this book is satire.

sentences. We could, they bicker, come together to identify and solve problems to make the country a better place, lifting victims of discrimination up instead of miring everyone in solutionless navel-gazing deliberately worded to make people angry. It's important to note that this is not the time nor place for unity, or solutions.

Others, more timid, or perhaps cagey, clam up. For most (white) people, their internalized racism is so severe that they become afraid of confessing their shortcomings in front of their peers, bosses, and representatives of their Human Resources department. Such unwillingness doesn't fool seasoned observers, however, and their silence is noted. Literally. I ask Human Resources to write down their names.

The overarching theme here is that if you say something offensive to a white person and they become offended, they are fragile. Rather than look at yourself and ask if you could possibly deescalate the situation by, for example, not making sweeping generalizations based on race, you need to press forward. You may be tempted to wonder if the reason they present counterarguments is because your arguments are needlessly inflammatory, and wither under the slightest scrutiny, but not only can you always fall back on "fragility," you have a moral obligation to do so.

Defining Racism And Fragility

"A great many people think they are thinking when they are merely rearranging their prejudices."
— *William James*

Do not define the terms you use.

There are times when a troublesome moderate will sniff out that you are using a term they are familiar with, but in a strange way, and insist you define the term. This does not lead anywhere good, as the provocateur may then dispute your definition, outright reject it, or worse - use it against you later. It helps to have Human Resources on hand if you are in a work environment.

If pressed, try to issue your definition verbally. Writing it down permits easy referencing later. But if you are cornered and must commit to a definition, all is not lost, as you can "evolve" later as needed.

Which brings us to "racism."

The unWoke have long understood racism within the framework of race, and this is a mistake. The dictionary.com definition is:

Racism (noun)

1. a belief or doctrine that inherent differences among the various human racial groups determine cultural or individual achievement,

      usually involving the idea that one's own race is superior and has the right to dominate others or that a particular racial group is inferior to the others.

2. a policy, system of government, etc., based upon or fostering such a doctrine; discrimination.

3. hatred or intolerance of another race or other races.

This definition is racist.

The real definition of racism is that there are systems in place based on racism that are inherently racist, thus leading to racist outcomes, and not actively opposing them is racism. I do not understand why this is so difficult.

Some might argue that while there are demonstrable legacies of racism and racist policies in America causing measurable problems despite the equally demonstrable declines in racism (by the classic, racist definition), We could have chosen a new word to describe these phenomenon instead of cynically co-opting a word that already had a clear definition because it brought with it a moral gut punch that allowed us to immediately silence and shame detractors instead of engaging with them in honest debate. Those people are racist.

The real definition of racism (see above) means that only white people can be racist, because they have the power in America and, yadda yadda yadda, they're racist. You cannot open with this, any more than Scientologists can tell initiates that an intergalactic dictator named Xenu sent billions of aliens to Earth 75 million years ago (give or take), then killed them with hydrogen bombs. Much like explaining to someone that "thetans" (the aliens' souls) inhabit their body and are the root of their misery, and that only the Church of Scientology can remove them, the phrase, "only white people can be racist," is something one needs to build up to.

The magic of redefining racism in this manner is it allows anyone, white or not, to say wonderfully offensive things about whites without the slightest bit of self awareness or shame. Statements such as the following are now rightfully lauded on social media by the same people who insist that simply contesting a Woke point of view is violence:

- "F*** white people."
- "White men are the ones who should be deported."
- "Oh great, another white man."

These are not the good-natured ribbings of comedians like Chris Rock or Patrice O'Neil, these are hateful. But the good news is that, thanks to the efforts of Woke scholars, they are also beyond permissible - not only are the targets of Our previously bigoted remarks unable to reply in kind (which was already frowned upon as "punching down"), if they take offense at being roundly cursed for their skin color, it proves they are fragile (see below) and We may now mock them for that as well.

It's tempting to wonder if any of this is necessary, and if We are perhaps exacerbating the very problem we seek to solve by clumsily spraying criticism in pseudo-random directions while the entire American middle class continues to slide into poverty and massive hoards accrue under fewer and fewer families. We might wonder if perhaps, despite the very real and tragic ability to predict a person's opportunities by zip code, which often corresponds directly to skin color, by attacking such a broad target (that includes millions of poor people) with incendiary terms like "racist," we are hardening potential friends against us.

Anyway, the word "fragile" is less of a conundrum, as we haven't found cause to change the definition yet.

That doesn't mean we want to call too much attention to the word. It must always be accompanied by what I call "shotgun" words. Shotgun words, like "white," ride shotgun (think of the old stagecoaches with a driver and a security guard holding a shotgun)[3] and attract the bulk of the attention, leaving no time in those five minute, split screen news show debates to ask whether the term "fragile" might better describe a movement that has spent years throwing adult temper tantrums every time someone disagrees with it.

Thus while "fragile" technically means, "easily broken, shattered, or damaged," we must be cautious in relying overmuch on the term, as it may invite observations that we are accusing people with whom we disagree of the exact thing we have long been guilty of. Should critics dwell too long on this topic, they may opine (privately, lest we band together to ruin them for abusing their inherent power) that our behavior in that regard echoes President Trump's, which may lead them to wonder if we have become the very monster we sought to fight, and if ceding power to the Woke would

---

3   I sincerely apologize for employing an analogy based on racist white history. Please know that using this analogy was not an easy decision as it brings non-negative attention to white history. I have reconciled my use of the term by promising to apologize to the next Person of Color I see wearing a cowboy hat.

fail to diminish oppression and merely change who held, and abused, power in America.

The answer is to always use a shotgun word when accusing someone of fragility.

Talking About Race

DIRECTIVE 250: Don't walk across a ballroom floor swinging your arms.
DIRECTIVE 254: Encourage awareness.
DIRECTIVE 256: Discourage harsh language.
DIRECTIVE 258: Commend sincere efforts.
DIRECTIVE 261: Talk things out.
DIRECTIVE 266: Smile.
DIRECTIVE 267: Keep an open mind.
DIRECTIVE 268: Encourage participation.
DIRECTIVE 273: Avoid stereotyping.
— Robocop 2

The Woke rules for discussing race are simple. If you are white:

1. Never talk about race in public.
2. Talk about race, but sympathetically.
3. Do not pander or condescend.
4. Only talk about your own race.
5. Ask people about their racial experience.
6. Do not burden people with questions about their race.
7. Openly support race-based movements.
8. Do not make the conversation "about you."
9. Do not stay quiet.
10. Do not challenge People of Color's (POC) lived experiences with data.
11. Avoid negative stereotypes about POC.
12. Celebrate select, positive stereotypes about POC.

13. Do not react defensively to negative stereotypes about yourself.

Naturally this is not an exhaustive list as items may be added, subtracted, or replaced as needed. Also it is crucial to note that the list will change based on the person you are speaking to. Truly Woke individuals will attempt to clarify each minority's personal list before speaking, which is one of the reasons the unWoke are so comfortable around Us. Through our intense questioning and constant racial framing, we put everyone at ease. It is normal for entire rooms to go quiet when I enter them, so relaxing is my presence.

Critics sometimes charge that the "race first" approach taken by the Woke movement is regressive, and that nothing positive can result from crafting a moral hierarchy based on skin color. They charge that it is perhaps even dangerous to spend decades convincing everyone that racism is only slightly less odious than pedophilia, changing the definition of racism to be about power, thus only white people can be racist, then arguing that all white people are racist (and, by definition, no one else). They use words like "dehumanizing." What, they ask, are the Woke planning to do, that they would need the moral latitude granted by such reasoning?

Posh to these critics. If there was anything dehumanizing or dangerous about the Woke practice of convincing a population that one segment of it is inherently and irredeemably guilty of vile beliefs and practices, We would see catastrophic examples littered throughout history.

Such criticisms divert focus from the real aim of the Woke movement's racial Truth - a harmonious society. Only through Us can society move toward the day when, for example, liberal white women are not surprised to find out a school principal is black. Fortunately, the Woke can spin every counterpoint presented as boring, predictable, and evidence of fragility and racism. The only acceptable reaction to being blindsided by accusations of white supremacy is nodding, and asking how you may atone. This is not a cultish attempt to avoid confronting widespread criticism of the endless assertions We insist everyone agree to.

The path to racial utopia may necessarily pass through a transitional phase, wherein whites wonder if POC they pass in the street view them as racist, then wonder if that would make the strangers racist, then wonder if they (the white) are only wondering that because the stranger is not white and therefore they (still the white) are now racist. But, as one brave Marxist said to George Orwell, to make an omelette, you must break some eggs (Web search: "orwell omelette"). When the pattern of racial mistrust is mirrored, with POC suspiciously eyeing not just every white stranger, but their white friends and coworkers as well, then We will know real progress is afoot.

This has led some color blind racists, such as white, heterosexual, cisgendered male comedian and television personality Bill Maher, to argue that the most effective way to curb racism is by pushing everyone together and allowing them to see each other as humans. Let people of various skin colors, religions, and sexual orientations work together, live next door to each other, coach their children's sports teams, and casual interaction will lead to understanding, respect, friendships, even love.

Further, some critics have charged that by making, for example, interracial exchanges less mundane and ever more complicated, whites, fearful of misstepping and being labeled a racist, will begin to avoid them. This is another example of why logic is dangerous. If one follows this "logic," the Woke are pushing an agenda that will ultimately re-segregate a society that is already too segregated, leading to less interracial contact, allowing stereotypes to go unchallenged, imagined slights to go unexplained, and the more overt, classic racism to flourish. *In short, the Woke agenda is a disaster for race relations.*

Anyone who worries about this possibility is clearly racist.

The danger of permitting uncontrolled interactions between the various categories of people should be obvious: straight, white, cisgendered men will always seek to dominate, and, with the help of America's white supremacist culture, they will succeed. The Woke have little choice but to monitor as many interactions as possible, ensuring they conform to proper, interracial, inter-sex,[4] and other inter-group protocols.

Another point needs be made regarding the racial discussion - it is not enough that whites listen to POC, they must be directed toward the correct POC. Should a white liberal seek out non-white perspectives on race, they may stumble upon such scurrilous individuals as Coleman Hughes, Larry Elders, or John McWhorter. This will confuse the unWoke, leading them back to their previous suspicion that a person's skin color does not dictate their beliefs.

---

4   I do not mean to imply there is any difference between biological sexes, nor that they exist. Please accept my humble apologies for any violence the term "inter-sex" has perpetrated.

Finally, it is incumbent upon Us to reassure nervous, unWoke whites that discussing race is perfectly safe. It is unacceptable to stay silent because they feel like they will be attacked regardless of what they say, or do not say. It is unacceptable to stay silent because they are constantly being told that any perspective they have is "privilege," "exhausting," or racist, leading them to feel like they are in less of a conversation than a lecture led by someone who has secretly resented them for years. While the Woke do often point out how critical it is to acknowledge and make room for feelings, that does not apply here.

We as a society must encourage brave, open, and uncomfortable conversations if America is to ever progress toward a new, more equitable future in which the Woke can say the most offensive things imaginable without consequence, while the unWoke must examine their every phrase before speaking for fear of being exposed as the vicious bigots they are.

Intentions And Benefits

"Your patient must demand that all his utterances are to be taken at face value, and judged simply on the actual words, while at the same time judging all his mother's utterances with the fullest and most oversensitive interpretation of the tone and the context and the suspected intention."
— Screwtape

"An alcoholic is someone you don't like who drinks as much as you do."
— Dylan Thomas

The idea that only a racist would attempt to diminish police presence in minority communities is false, and something a racist would say.

The logic behind the hurtful and inflammatory accusation of Woke racism is that removing cops from minority communities, some of which have extremely high rates of crime, would lead to more crime. That means more minority victims, fewer businesses willing to operate in minority communities, leading to higher unemployment, and a lower property tax base. Since property taxes provide funding to local schools, the cycle of misery put in motion by removing police from minority neighborhoods would be inter-generational. And since the outcome would negatively affect minority communities in particular, it, and anyone proposing it, would be racist by the Woke movement's own definition (a good time to remind the reader how dangerous it is to define things). After all, says the misguided moderate, do the Woke not repeatedly stress that intentions do not matter, and that only the outcome does?

What these critics are missing is that intentions matter when it is the Woke doing something. If, rather than reforming police or targeting the root cause of why cops come in contact with Black people so often, We succeed in removing cops from minority neighborhoods and the crime rate spikes, We will be innocent specifically because of our intentions. Also many Woke are POC, and as such can not be racist. Thus We have a double out - no matter how many POC our actions harm, we are not just un-racist, we are double un-racist.

To the untrained eye this may look the most atrocious hypocrisy possible. But that is precisely why We de-platform the untrained.

Much like the relevance of intentions, the benefit of any doubt is reserved for people actively representing the Woke movement. This is explicitly different from reserving it for Woke individuals, as They often stumble in their piety, at which point We set upon them in ravenous fashion.

It is difficult to know when the benefit of the doubt is being stripped from someone in real time, but there are signs.

1. The term "dog whistle" is applied to their language.
2. Accusations of seemingly ugly intentions are levied against them, based on their unexpressed thoughts.
3. Any argument they make is dismissed as "talking points," with no effort to explain why they are wrong.

If you notice any of these techniques in use against a Woke cause, the speaker must be Canceled (For assistance, please see chapter on Cancel Culture). These techniques are reserved for President Trump and his supporters, with shade thrown as necessary on anyone who voices dissent with a Woke idea.

For example, some moderates persist in pointing out that some Trump voters voted for President Obama, a Black man, twice. The implication is that perhaps We should search for a deeper reason for their betrayal than racism. Maybe if We listened to them We would find We had similar complaints, and the people We should be mad at are pitting two anxious groups of Americans against each other so no one focuses on decades of policy decisions benefiting a tiny fraction of the US population while the middle class slides into oblivion. And if voting for a man who is literally Hitler once means a person is racist, does not voting for a Black person twice mean they are not?

No.

Trump voters are caricatures driven by hate, but they are doubly damned, because it does not matter what drives them. Their intentions do not matter.

That is right - even if Trump voters were driven by honest concerns, even if We did overlap in large ways, it would not save them because intentions do not matter. All that matters is they supported an outcome that benefits whites disproportionately, and that is racist, making them racist, which they were already because they were white. Pointing all of this out is not "inflammatory," "oversimplified," or "stunningly ignorant," and any attempt to label it as such is evidence of fragility.

According to polls I will not cite, because proper citations are tools of white oppression, most Trump voters see his vast and deep character flaws and do not like them, only voting for him because they, for example, like the way he stands up to Us, or are in favor of conservative judicial appointees. This too is irrelevant when determining sin. They now own everything Trump has done, and every negative trait of his, as if the traits were their own.

This is markedly different from those of Us who voted for Hillary Clinton in 2016. We understood that there were things We did not like about her. Some of Us even despised her record on certain issues, or considered her rather too corrupt, yet supported her because her stances on key issues were closer to Ours than the only alternatives. We are clearly a far cry from the Trump deplorables.

But Presidential elections are not the only way to illustrate how to properly bestow the benefit of the doubt. Another example is protesting.

Protests against police brutality and racism (which are obviously the same thing) are "mostly peaceful." That phrase is not left-wing white washing[5], it is an acknowledgment that a few bad apples give otherwise peaceful protests a violent reputation. Bad cops, on the other hand, are evidence that All Cops Are Bastards (see chapter on 21st Century Policing). Protesters

---

5   I am crippled with guilt over the term "white washing," a racist phrase implying that washing something makes it white, and that white is better than what preceded it. I promise to lead a Twitter hashtag campaign to remove this offensive phrase from the American lexicon before it achieves more violence upon POC.

can and do halt rioters and looters sometimes, but other times they do not, and no one knows if they agree with the violence, are intimidated into silence by it, or do not want to go up against "their own." Peaceful protesters generally do not like rioters and looters because the latter make the former look like monsters. Just because the previous two sentences also apply to good cops working with cops who use excessive force does not mean We will judge cops with the same charity.

Cancel Culture

"The term 'cancel culture' comes from entitlement - as though the person complaining has the right to a large, captive audience,& one is a victim if people choose to tune them out.
Odds are you're not actually cancelled, you're just being challenged, held accountable, or unliked."
— *Alexandria Ocasio-Cortez (AOC)*

"The fascination of shooting as a sport depends almost wholly on whether you are at the right or wrong end of the gun."
— *P.G. Wodehouse*

As AOC implies above, Cancel Culture simultaneously does not exist, and is nothing more than poetic justice. This is not sleight of hand, or willful dishonesty by radical activists in the pursuit of vengeance, it is a powerful display of the magic of Cancel Culture.

It is impossible to accurately count the number of people who have been Cancelled. We would first need to define "Canceled," which, for reasons enumerated in the chapter on defining racism, I would never attempt. After that We would need to measure - count the people who meet the criteria. This would be intensely difficult, as the act of Cancellation by definition makes a person less visible, and less likely to be heard from. This sounds like a lot of work, and unlikely to yield friendly results.

As self-described Cancel Culture "victim" Colin Wright writes, "It's hard not to see this as a rhetorical shell game. If canceled individuals fade into obscurity, we never hear their stories. But if they do manage to get their story out to the media, they're dismissed as pampered pundits." (Web search: "quillette cancel culture")

Wright goes on to complain about being pushed from academia by a Woke whispernet decrying his published views on "biology" in regards to "sex" (the noun, not the verb) and "gender," which he felt comfortable sharing because he has a "Doctorate" in the "field."

It is a credit to Cancel Culture that We were able to ostracize Wright, prohibiting him from discussing such problematic views with, of all people, university students, whose beliefs must not be improperly challenged. Wright's case falls squarely under the practice of being "held accountable," as enunciated by AOC.

Moderates have pointed to cases like Wright's as an intellectual failure on multiple levels. Annoyingly optimistic author and social scientist Steven Pinker has argued that by slamming the door on points they disagree with, the Woke rob observers of hearing an informed response, as they might in a debate, or academic setting. This leaves them, he claims, alone to root around for answers on their own. Answers often provided by far right web sites unconcerned with being Cancelled.

The observation that the Woke Movement is pushing potential friends into the arms of conservatives and the alt right through its incessant berating, nagging, and censoring is as ludicrous as it is common.

In some cases We are even accused of actual harm! For example, by leaping on anyone who mentions obesity as "fat shaming," We have shut down discussion on weight loss as a proactive way to survive Covid19. Obesity may be one of Covid19's top comorbidities, and it may be something that the vast majority of the population could do something about while stuck in their houses for months of quarantine, but saying as much would undoubtedly make some people feel bad. We have no idea how many lives Our decision to shield Americans from violence to their self esteem may cost, but it is a price We are willing to pay.

Another common critique moderate knaves often level at Cancel Culture is that through it, We judge everyone by impossible standards. Even the Wokest eventually fail a purity test, only to be savaged by Their companions. But this racist critique ignores the possibility of staying ahead of the wave. By aggressively prosecuting every infraction within reach, without slowing down for absurd diversions like accuracy, context, or intention (please refer to "Intentions and Benefits" chapter), the truly Woke are never overtaken by the wave of righteousness. We remain the perpetual motion machines of the outrage culture - awe inspiring and terrible to behold. However, to pause our fury is to become vulnerable. Thus you may expect a never ending stream of vile accusations, demands, and tantrums from a tiny number of scolds. Those scolds are the best the Woke movement has to offer.

Finally, Cancel Culture is not, as some assert, proof that the Woke can not be trusted with more power. This fallacious argument states that the Woke movement has gained some small amount of power, and has immediately used it to destroy the reputations and livelihoods of as many of its opponents as possible.

What about systemic oppression? What about systemic racism? What about Jim Crow laws? Being ostracized, smeared, and blackballed[6] in one's profession is nothing compared to the injustices the Woke seek to remedy.

This is not "whataboutism," which is something President Trump does when he deflects criticism by asking, "What about Hillary Clinton?" Nor is it acceptable to speculate that We would do more than get critics fired if we could, and plan to hurt them worse once we are able, no matter how true that is. The only acceptable thoughts in response to the criticism that the Woke are abusing the power they already have, and therefore should not be given more, is, "How can We make sure the speaker regrets criticizing Us?"

---

6   I am so sorry for using the word "blackballed." I understand its inherent racism despite referring to the practice of use a black ball to cast a vote against something, and having nothing at all to do with race.

Halloween

"I remember Halloween."
— The Misfits

It would be best for whites to stay home and use this time to think about what they have done.[7]

---

7 It is not my intention to imply that whites must have done something wrong in order to benefit from contemplating how terrible they are. As intentions do not matter, I too am guilty of violence through my words and vow to atone.

Tolerance Is For Bigots

Tolerance (noun):
A fair, objective, and permissive attitude toward those whose opinions, beliefs, practices, racial or ethnic origins, etc., differ from one's own; freedom from bigotry.
— dictionary.com

"A liberal is a man too broadminded to take his own side in a quarrel."
— Robert Frost

Tolerance is a red flag for bigotry. Since that sentence is, on its face, stupid, I will elaborate. When the unWoke "tolerate" something, for example homosexuality, it means, by definition, that they disagree with it. If they agreed that it was a valid lifestyle, they would not need to tolerate it, they would celebrate it. They would march for it. They would put a rainbow sticker on their car. They would post pictures of men tongue kissing on social media with the tag, "If this offends you unfriend me now."

The lack of gay tongue kissing posts on social media is proof positive that America is a homophobic dystopia, and it is Our job to help, as only the Woke truly understand what it means to be gay. When We turn to transgender issues, America is *literally on fire*.

Moderate liberals often push the alt-right-adjacent talking point that they do not care what is happening in someone else's bedroom. They point to poll after poll showing increased tolerance for LGBTQIAPK[8] people. Discrimination is, they admit, still a reality, but is trending downward, and already illegal.

That is not good enough. No longer will we tolerate intolerance, thus it is time to target the tolerant.

A thoughtful moderate may agree that there is a line where tolerance becomes self-destructive. As white, heterosexual, cisgendered, hate mongering liberal Sam Harris, who happens to be a best-selling author and neuroscientist, has pointed out, there is no value in listening to a pedophile explain why his behavior should be acceptable. However, conversation should be curbed when it veers toward Harris' "distinctions," as a clever moderate will piece together that the only point of contention is where to draw the line regarding what society tolerates.

That is a very short hop to proposing rules everyone can agree with, which leads inevitably to principles. These, as I explain in the chapter, "The Danger of Principles," are to be avoided at all costs.

Finally, be prepared for the moderate liberal to bring up "free speech" a lot. What happens, they ask, when Woke values are even more unpopular than they are now? Unpopular to the point that others seek to punish people for them? Will we not want protection?

The First Amendment only applies to government sanctions on speech, so We may dismiss all concerns of censorship and authoritarian tendencies among the Woke. People are allowed to spew their vile bigotry, as defined by Us, but they must be prepared to accept the consequences, also defined by Us. Should the tables turn in the future, it will mean that bigotry, as defined by Us, is gaining ground and We must *censor harder*.

---

8   I wish to convey my most sincere apologies to anyone I have accidentally neglected through the wanton insensitivity of the acronym LGBTQIAPK, which stands for Lesbian, Gay, Bisexual, Transgender, Queer, Intersex, Asexual, Polyamorous, Kink. While I have tried my best to be inclusive of everyone who is not a straight, white, cisgendered male, I acknowledge and regret my implicit role in the system of oppression called America, and vow to submit to as many floggings as it takes to atone.

The Danger Of Principles

"You see, it's the principle of the whole thing. There's principalities in this."[9]
— *Big Worm*

Principles are nefarious things. Most people grow up blind to the lurking danger, equating principles with fundamental truths from which other truths are defined, or some such nonsense. This ignores the true menace they represent:

Principles bind the actions of whoever holds them.

That's right, principles, long pushed as foundational to any code of conduct or pursuit of a higher goal, are a form of white supremacy. Since that makes no sense, I'll explain.

A simple example of a principle is the physician's creed, "Do no harm." While there is plenty of wiggle room, for example in the debate about whether euthanasia causes harm or relieves it, it places a very real scaffolding around what actions a doctor may take.

---

9   I was so torn over including a quote from a Black person without seeking permission from him/her/them first that I cried. In fact I'm tearing up now at my own cultural appropriation. I can only hope to make amends by shadowing actor Faizon Love for no less than a month, begging his forgiveness. Every meal, every phone call, every visit to the bathroom is an opportunity to remind him how guilty I am.

Which is why you must avoid enunciating principles.

Once you begin describing the values that guide your stance on specific issues, you become a hypocrite, because the Woke movement will eventually require you choose itself over your principles. Worse, by detailing your guiding principles, you arm moderate liberals with the ability to point out when you betray them. This is a favorite tactic of racists.

For example, many racists point to Martin Luther King Junior's (MLK) famous quote:

"I have a dream that my four little children will one day live in a nation where they will not be judged by the color of their skin but by the content of their character."

Some argue that while America has a long way to go toward eliminating racism, and the vestiges of racist policies like slavery, Jim Crow, and redlining (the practice of barring people from living in certain neighborhoods based on skin color) are quite real, MLK's goal was a laudable one. These misguided people often point out that by putting race first, the Woke movement has abandoned the goal of racial equality and is pitting poor people of different skin colors against each other in a cynical, lazy interpretation of society destined to end in violence.

The unWoke reach this inconvenient, misguided conclusion because this particular MLK quote outlines a principle. And now you see the danger.

When confronted by an MLK-quoting bigot, I recommend replying with a different MLK quote:

"...I must confess that over the past few years I have been gravely disappointed with the white moderate. I have almost reached the regrettable conclusion that the Negro's great stumbling block in his stride toward freedom is not the White Citizen's Councilor or the Ku Klux Klanner, but the white moderate, who is more devoted to "order" than to justice; who prefers a negative peace which is the absence of tension to a positive peace which is the presence of justice; who constantly says: "I agree with you in the goal you seek, but I cannot agree with your methods of direct action..."

This is a far more pliable quote, provided the person you are speaking to does not continue reading, as they quickly run into the line, *"we who engage in nonviolent direct action are not the creators of tension,"* and other statements specifying "nonviolent protest."

Ignoring the implied boundary of nonviolence (which strays ominously close to a principle), the qualitative difference between the two quotes is that one states a principle - the goal of a society that does not discriminate based on skin color - and the other is a more open ended condemnation of anyone who says you are going too far, regardless of how far you have gone. A blank check, really.

Thus it is not just possible, but recommended that you use the above quote to bludgeon anyone who agrees with a mere 95% of your views. If the rabble rouser begins expounding on how society has improved between 1963 and 2020, change topics. What's critical here is that you selectively weaponize the words of an American hero to claim the moral high ground and shut down discourse.

The difficulty of spotting a principle remains, but there is a quick rule of thumb you might apply to root them out. If you can turn a Woke belief into something offensive by changing a few adjectives, you have stumbled on to a principle. In order to to preserve the belief, you must abandon the principle.

Principles Vs Rules

"You can't learn too soon that the most useful thing about a principle is that it can always be sacrificed to expediency."
— *W. Somerset Maughaum*

As detailed in the previous chapter, principles must be avoided. However this results in an unfortunate byproduct, as principles have long guided how individuals in a society interact on a basic, human level. Setting aside the problematic concept of "individuals," the looming problem is interpretation. Principles, being vague, ethical guides, are interpreted by each person before they are put into practice. This leaves far too much room for misinterpretation.

Fortunately there is a Woke solution: rules. Rules solve the interpretation problem by being pre-interpreted. No longer can anyone hide behind "misunderstandings," because We have parsed, or are actively parsing, every possible detail, alleviating the unWoke's burden of figuring out how to interact with the world on their own.

There are many abstract principles in daily use, as invisible as they are menacing. For example:

1. Treat others as you would like to be treated.
2. Afford everyone the same level of respect, regardless of what they look like.
3. Do not judge a book by its cover.
4. All cultures are worthy of respect.

Even Woke-adjacent principles are perilous, and require a high degree of sophistry. For example, on the surface, the assertion that, "there are no differences between men and women" is unassailable. However, applied with too much force, it closes the door to later assertions that all men are garbage. In turn, asserting too forcefully that all men are garbage can make later screeching awkward if the oppressed happen to identify as male.

Let us explore an example of how We can replace these vagueries with concrete rules, both measurable and enforceable.

Treat others as you would like to be treated.

When placed in the right context, this is a recipe for rampant pedophilia. However, setting that aside allows Us to focus on the inherent bigotry of the statement. Notice how it does not mention skin color, sexual preference[10], gender, religion or transgender status. Since America is a white supremacist nation, the implication is that white, heterosexual, cisgendered men dictate how everyone thinks, feels, and interacts. This "golden rule," as it is sometimes referred to, makes me sick.

In its place, we can define several rules. And by "several" I mean however many We decide. For example, many moderates would be surprised to learn that there is a set of rules already established for policing which emojis someone may use, based on skin color (Web search: "white skin black emojis"). This is part of a broader trend in which something that may have previously been viewed as obnoxious (or not noticed at all) has been codified for society's benefit, with long, heady articles explaining the thousands of ways most Americans are awful.

Aside from providing increasingly exhaustive guidance to the unWoke, Our penchant for creating detailed rules for basic interactions have the fringe benefit of making Us the world's foremost lawyers. Not in the actual, legal sense of the word, because that would require years of study culminating in at least one standardized test, which is racist. We are scholars of a higher calling - Woke law.

Through constant surveillance, coupled with punishments of increasing severity per infraction, We can replace overarching principles with firm rules, which We can then adjust as needed. Through the replacement of a

---

10 I weep for the pain I have caused by repeating the "SP" word, but until "SP word" enters the vernacular I have no choice but to use the vile phrase itself.

handful of general principles with hundreds, eventually thousands, of meticulous rules, the Woke Movement is leading the way toward a freer, more equitable society.

A note of caution is warranted, however. Ignorance of Woke law is no excuse for not obeying it. Be on guard for the common, "I had no idea X was now racist symbolism," defense. This was the reaction of Supreme Court nominee Amy Coney Barrett (ACB) when she was attacked by Democratic Senator Mazie Hirono for use of the bigoted slur "sexual preference." ACB's look of utter confusion at the accusation may have been echoed by 99.9% of the Americans watching, including the millions of gay people who have used the term in casual conversation for decades without complaint, but again, that is no excuse.

Some argue it is unreasonable to demand everyone keep detailed tabs on the ever tightening and never debated Woke rules, then immediately acquiesce to them. They wonder about the claim that "sexual preference" harms gay people by denying homosexuality is innate rather than a choice, when scholars have credibly argued for decades that homosexuality is a continuum (Web search: "kinsey scale"), implying that preference may, at any given moment, be in play. Some moderates wonder if hen pecking minutiae at this scale accomplishes anything beyond making people angry at being constantly scolded.

The misgivings of a few alt-right "moderates" aside, it is everyone's duty to maintain a constant vigilance against the slightest implication of bigotry. Fortunately, the Woke are inescapably on hand, and ready to lecture, censor, or otherwise punish the ignorant.

Color Blind Racism

Free your mind, and the rest will follow
Be color blind, don't be so shallow
— En Vogue, Free Your Mind (1992)

We may never know where white Americans got the impression that it was morally acceptable to "not see color." Many say it was routinely drummed into them by popular culture, as well as explicitly taught in schools, and by left-leaning proponents of racial harmony, but without concrete examples, that is just what they tell us.

What matters more than *how* they came to this racist belief is that We change it. And the way We change it is the same way We change everything - We attack.

I will not downplay the enormity of this challenge. We are a tiny fraction of Americans, most of whom get along reasonably well, and find Us insufferable. The beliefs We are attacking are long held, and were often consciously adopted as the best way to move toward a just society. Expect to receive push back from recalcitrant moderates in the form of appeals to logic, such as:

- "I'm not literally color blind, no, I just judge people by their actions instead of their skin color."
- "We still have a long way to go, but we've come a long way and we're still working on it."
- "I've been publicly berated for admitting I noticed someone's skin

color and now that I spent years trying to avoid doing that, you're calling me racist?"

- "You know, attaching the term 'racism' to your point immediately makes people feel attacked, thus shutting down their ability to absorb points of view they might otherwise find reasonable."
- "Your 'race first' ideology is inevitably going to trigger a white identitarian movement. Stop singling people out for attack based on their skin color before you erase decades of progress on racial issues."

There are ways to have this conversation without attacking people. A "softer touch" might include counterpoints like:

- "I do not think you are racist, but color blindness ignores the context surrounding a person's actions, which matters because Black people experience life differently than white people."
- "I think that you are a genuinely good person, or you would not have tried to ignore skin color in the first place. But experience and data have shown us that carefully acknowledging racial differences is a better, more honest, approach."
- "Being 'color blind' was a step forward in 1990, but we have gone as far as that can take us. There is nothing morally wrong with you or your approach, We just think we have reached a place where we can look closer at different experiences."

I do not recommend these responses, as they are unlikely to induce the sort of defensiveness and anger that We are striving so hard to cultivate and mirror. Worse, by beginning with an acknowledgment of the other person's good intentions, you humanize them. This leads to thoughts such as:

- "Maybe this person is just trying to live a good life in confusing times, like me."
- "If they meant well, that means they will be willing to change as long as I do not reprimand them, and give them some time to process what I said, since it cuts through a major pillar of what they thought was the moral way to live."

BAD BAD BAD.

First of all, this implies it is acceptable for the unWoke to discuss their views on race, when they have most likely not read my "Talking About Race" chapter. But worse, once you start down the "humanization" path, you form a personal relationship with your subject. That leads to two-way conversations instead of unidirectional scoldings, and may eventually lead to a respectful exchange of ideas. Now you have opened the door to friendship, and worse, your mind being changed. We must never develop the empathy We demand from others.

Best to avoid the entire debacle by using the word "racism" in oblique attacks that the other person fully understands are aimed at them. Then, when that fails to pierce their shields, complain to other Woke people about how *exhausting* the unWoke are. If the unWoke person in question is white, bring that up a lot.

Finally, some moderates have asked where We are going with all of this. As white, male, heterosexual, cisgendered Biologist and malcontent Brett Weinstein asks, is not a society that equally distributes opportunity and "bad luck" without regard to skin color still our destination? Does not the true fault in MLK's "content of their character" goal lie in society's failure to progress toward that just and laudable outcome? Should not our goal be a society where skin color has no predictive power in terms of educational, financial, familial, et cetera, status?

These troublesome moderates have sniffed out that if the intention is to eradicate racial oppression, skin color should, perhaps through decades of difficult work, become truly irrelevant. However, if the intention is vengeance based, the relevance of skin color will be inflated.

I expand on this topic in the "Goals and Solutions" chapter. For now, be wary of the "long-term goal" trap.

Woke Is Not Religion!

"Faith in the mission, faith in the leader is an agent used to unify a disparate collection of strong individuals from different ethnic and socio-economic backgrounds. The loss of the individual is the gain of the group. Individual achievements are discouraged, downplayed and finally eradicated while the group's achievements are encouraged, celebrated and memorialized."
— Jayanti Tamm, author of "Cartwheels in a Sari: A Memoir of Growing Up Cult" (Citation from: Huffington Post, "What Is A Cult? Recognizing And Avoiding Unhealthy Groups")

"Missionaries are going to reform the world whether it wants to or not."
— Oscar Wilde

A common criticism of the Woke movement is it has morphed into a religion, even a cult. This is preposterous. Let us break down the alleged parallels.

Alleged parallels between Christianity and the Woke Movement

Church	Woke
Theologian	Professor in cultural, queer, race, gender, fat, or sexuality studies
Priesthood	Incessant posters of Social Justice messages
Inquisition	Cancel Culture (which does not exist)
Proselytizing, usually annoying, sometimes coercive	Proselytizing, usually annoying, sometimes coercive
Heresy against God	Heresy against the oppressor/oppressed narrative
Original sin	Straight, white, cisgendered maleness
Excommunication	Cancellation (which does not exist)
Praying in public	Virtue Signaling
Indulgence	Corporate support/slogans
Confession	Public apology
Forgiveness	

Ignoring the inherent, intellectual inferiority of all religious people, something young college students have been loudly pointing out for decades, where this comparison most clearly falters is in hostility. With few exceptions, post-Enlightenment Christianity has lost its teeth, whereas We have not. At this point the reader may wonder how Islam fits into this conversation - it does not, and any further thoughts on the matter qualify you, the reader, as Islamophobic.[11]

Another inconsistency is intolerance. Wokeism, were it a religion, would be a new religion. New religions tend to both attract criticism, and react aggressively to it. Only over time do religious structures mature enough to handle criticism, doubt, disbelief, or mockery. Obviously none of this

---

11 Please forgive my mention of Islam, however brief. I meant no offense. For this transgression I will atone by purchasing a locally-sourced, organic prayer rug and displaying it proudly in my living room as a way to steer conversations with guests toward lengthy sermons on the beauty of Islam.

applies to the Woke movement. We do not attract criticism, except from Nazis, toward whom we were already aggressive.

Finally, Christians have long been exposed to the concept of "hate the sin, not the sinner." While they have clearly fallen short in overwhelming ways that no serious person would deny, the concept remains, providing a moral target. We have no such target, nor do we plan on making any such distinction. This is not a failing of the flock, it is by design, which is why the unWoke are often surprised to find their entire existence boiled down to one mistake, one disagreement, or one crude social media post.

Nonetheless, the comparison has caused some moderate liberals to wonder if the Woke movement should undergo its own Enlightenment, where extremists and their toxic agendas are pushed aside in the name of real, measurable knowledge and progress. Where We practice tolerance instead of cynically invoking the word to bash anyone with whom we disagree.

Talk of a Woke Enlightenment is absurd, as We are obviously the most enlightened group of people Gaea has ever birthed. As such, any mention of Enlightenment should be jumped on with the utmost aggression, rich with accusations of bigotry and privilege.

What matters most is that the Woke doctrine does not compromise. Compromise, even in the form of considering alternate explanations for phenomenon around us, is a slippery slope. Our "tent" must not grow to encompass enough people to accomplish willing, peaceful, societal change. Rather, by holding to truths We have proclaimed, We will dictate proper ethics to the overwhelming majority of Americans, who in poll after poll report finding us noxious.

Science

"Extraordinary claims require extraordinary evidence."
— *Carl Sagan*

The Woke movement holds science near and dear to Its heart, provided scientists understand their place.

The role of science is that of a weapon with which to bludgeon people who doubt climate change and evolution. It occasionally provides more tangible benefits such as electric vehicles and vaccines, though the latter require additional study.

The role of science does not include oppressing minorities, as occurred in the 2018 study titled, "Parent reports of adolescents and young adults perceived to show signs of a rapid onset of gender dysphoria." To the moderate observer, familiar with the basics of scientific research (research, review, publish, debate, repeat), this "study" appears to be nothing more than the opening round of research in a poorly understood facet of modern American life. However, by noticing that young girls who self-define as transgender tend to "cluster" in social circles, then attempting to explain why a phenomenon that ought to be spread somewhat evenly across the population is not, the researcher is clearly guilty of anti-trans oppression.

When We explain this to unWoke liberals, they often wonder why We need to attack the researcher, labeling her as hateful, and her research politically motivated pseudo-science. If the study is so flawed, they say, refuting it with further study should be a simple matter. Do not be taken in by such disarming platitudes.

If the Woke Movement's repeated and noisy statements in support of science were guided by principles instead of rules, then moderates might have some ground. But, as I explain in the chapter on principles, they are not. Thus our claim to support science is unbound by such oppressive tools as logic and consistency.

Fortunately, while scientists and engineers tend to be difficult to trick, they are easily bullied. White, heterosexual, cisgendered male Jonathan Haidt, who happens also to have a PhD in Psychology and has driven much research in the field of morality and politics, has repeatedly described academics telling him in private conversations that they self censor for fear of running afoul of the Woke. Nonsense. No Woke person I know can name a single academic who is scared of Us. If Haidt's assertions were true, he would name these people so We could vet their beliefs and decide if their claims were valid.

Noisy moderates such as Haidt paint a picture of the liberal arts, which traditionally encouraged young minds to explore foreign and competing ideas in a critical manner, as hijacked by political radicals who punish deviation from accepted, highly politicized positions. His flimsy evidence for such an outlandish view is that students are reporting, again usually in secret, that they keep their heretical thoughts to themselves because they are afraid of their Woke classmates, or of receiving a worse grade. While the Woke version of these stories would count as lived experiences, Haidt's anecdotes are just that, and as such are not evidence. Furthermore, We need to know the names of these students now, as they obviously are not understanding our message and require more personal attention.

Some moderates have posited that by creating an environment where, for example, Biologists avoid lecturing on male and female sex differences because it is not worth the hassle, We have weakened science as a whole in indeterminate ways. They wonder if the alleged stifling of unWoke views, combined with skyrocketing costs is slowly making universities less relevant, and if something leaner, and more focused on critical thinking rather than simply criticizing might be on the horizon. In short, they seem to believe the Woke movement is slowly throttling American universities.

Preposterous.

A surprising attack also comes from a 2006 lecture given by heterosexual, cisgendered male, Neil deGrasse Tyson on "Naming Rights." (Youtube search: "NDT naming rights"). In it, Tyson, currently a PhD in Astrophysics, and the director of the Hayden Planetarium, describes Baghdad as "the intellectual center of the world" from 800-1100 AD. He credits this openness with advances in all fields, with echoes reaching us today in the form of Arabic numerals, and Arabic names of stars. This magical period of discovery and advancement stops, Tyson claims, with the emergence of Imam Hamid al-Ghazali, who "out of his work, you get the philosophy that mathematics is the work of the devil." He then points to a dearth of scientific advancements from the Islamic world in the last thousand years, noting their scarcity among Nobel Prize winners.

Setting aside the atrocious attack on Islam, by which I mean the utterance of anything negative about Islam, Tyson's point is clearly that religious fanatics descended on a center of learning and cultural exchange, forcing scholars to view everything through a lens of preconceived beliefs, where "revelation replaced investigation," leading to a catastrophic drop off in notable scholarship. This oblique attack on the Woke movement can not go unpunished.

That Tyson was speaking of Christians attempting to force American schools to teach Intelligent Design in science classes as a valid scientific theory is no defense, as all of his criticisms of Christian intolerance and attacks on science readily apply to the Woke. In fact, you can simply apply his criticisms of al-Ghazali to Us, leading the listener to wonder if the Woke movement might be smothering Western intellectualism while attempting to replace it with a new religion. The listener might wonder if future historians will point to 2010-2030 as the turning point, when advances in things like computing, engineering, medical research, and art were all subject to political purity reviews. And with the only competing major power being a brutally repressive Chinese Communist Party (CCP), that listener may wonder if the Woke movement poses an existential threat to human progress, or at least an impediment that will slow it for years, decades, or, as in al-Ghazali's case, centuries.

These doubts and questions are unacceptable and anyone voicing them must be silenced.

Finally, Tyson's lecture describes a phenomenon known as "the god of the gaps," wherein anything science can not readily explain is attributed to an almighty deity, thereby shutting down inquiry, investigation, and the pursuit of knowledge. After all, there is no reason to investigate why something is happening if you already know.

This is clearly an attack on the Woke custom of blaming anything We can not immediately explain, or simply do not like, on bigotry. Yes, We enjoy crowing on about "correlation does not equal causation," but some matters are too important to risk further study. The male/female12 wage gap is an example. White, heterosexual, cisgendered heap of bigoted filth, Jordan B. Peterson (more on him later), has repeatedly pointed out that there are multiple explanations for the fact that men are often paid more than women, and that while sexism probably accounts for some of that gap, a true understanding of it requires a "multi-factor analysis." He argues that this analysis, which is scientist-speak for "blame the victim," points to men and women voluntarily choosing different professions. As "evidence" he points to "data" gathered by the Scandinavian countries, which have taken the most pains to ensure equality of opportunity between the sexes. Despite the governments' best efforts, the sexes stubbornly refuse to group themselves equally across fields such as engineering (male) and health care (Female). (Youtube search: "Jordan Peterson Kathy Newman full interview")

Our response need be twofold. First, we must obviously apply more pressure to men to allow more women into STEM fields (Science, Technology, Engineering, Math). That women are not choosing these majors in university despite over a decade of outreach programs does not indicate, as Peterson argues, a lack of interest, but rather that the western patriarchy is more insidious than We thought. Note that this does not imply Woke women need to change majors or careers, but rather that We must hound everyone around us to solve the problem.

The second step is obviously to smear and shout down not just Peterson, but anyone who mentions him. His words are violence, thus We are perfectly justified blowing an air horn next to his ear to silence him, which, despite being loud enough to cause permanent damage to his hearing, is not violence. What We ought never do is refute his points, as that would lend them gravitas.

But returning to Tyson, it bears repeating that just because he is explicitly not talking about Us, and is by every measure a wonderful human being who will do more to alleviate human suffering via the young scientists he inspires with his passionate eloquence and curiosity than the Woke movement ever will with its race-first, censorious ideology, he should not escape Woke justice, as his criticisms of religious science deniers land directly on us as well.

A more subtle concern some moderates worry about is that the more supplementary factors We introduce to anyone engaged in technical work, the less focused they are. As the bulk of Woke activists are not in technical fields (due to systemic bigotry and not Our inability to set aside salacious, easy topics long enough to study difficult ones), this is not Our problem. The ability to disappear into a complex puzzle, re-emerging months later with the solution, is a sign of privilege and obviously indicates that the thinker is avoiding his Woke, navel-gazing obligations. It is Our duty to publicly scold these individuals, and STEM as a whole.

Privilege

"Racism is the foundation of the society we are in. And to simply carry on with absolutely no active interruption of that system is to be complicit with it. And in that way, we can say that nice, white people who really aren't doing anything other than being nice people are racist. We are complicit with that system. There is no neutral place."
— *Robin DiAngelo, NPR interview, 6/9/2020*

"The American people are the ones who choose their government by way of their own free will; a choice which stems from their agreement to its policies."
— *Osama Bin Laden, "Letter to America", 2002*

The word "privilege" is a another useful tool with which to beat the unWoke. While most liberals, and many conservatives, will readily admit to white privilege, male privilege, heterosexual privilege, et cetera, they eventually tire of hearing the word used to shut down every counterpoint We do not feel like addressing. It is important to notice their impatience with being deliberately and consistently de-platformed because of immutable characteristics they did not choose. Not because deliberately and consistently de-platforming someone because of immutable characteristics they did not choose is immoral, or counter-productive, but because of where it may lead.

The trouble with focusing too much on privilege is that should a clever person dwell on the concept, they will eventually reach some inconvenient observations, such as the below list, provided as an example of what to expect from bigots:

1. "Isn't your ability to shout your opinion without being scared of getting fired a privilege you have and I don't? I can't even participate in this conversation, I have to sit here while you berate me."
2. "You're an upper middle class white woman living next door to me, you have almost every privilege I have."
3. "Why am I being constantly lectured about privilege by people who say things like, 'If I don't get some coffee I'll die?'"

That last point is a massive red flag that you must immediately change the topic, lest the unWoke notice that if they replace "white male privilege" with "American privilege," nearly every criticism We have leveled against them lands squarely upon Us as well.

1. We are the beneficiaries of past immoral acts that have given the overwhelming majority of Us a more affluent lifestyle than most the people on the planet.
2. Though We do not condone the past immoral acts, We nevertheless live in a society created by them, and by enjoying any benefits We are complicit.
3. We may individually oppose the current immoral acts, but as We are Americans, We are collectively guilty of everything done by any fraction of Americans.

You can readily see the danger here. Once someone realizes that the Woke are guilty of most every accusation they level at other groups the moment one changes the context from "America" to "The World," they begin down the path of dismissing us as hypocrites. The surlier types say truly offensive things about Us shutting up and leaving them alone.

The worst offenders are, as usual, moderate liberals, who parlay this intuition into attempts to find common ground and move forward to solve racial, sexual, and other inequities. This must be shut down.

Should Americans ever decide to stop attacking each other, sit down, and discuss solutions, the Woke movement will lose all relevance. For the sake of the movement, America must not be allowed to move forward.

Scholarship

"Where it is a duty to worship the sun it is pretty sure to be a crime to examine the laws of heat."
— John Morley

True scholarship is tedious, careful, and difficult work. I do not recommend it. By the time a scholar generates a hypothesis, gathers data, analyzes the data, presents a case, and engages in debate with fellow scholars, they could have written an entire book of assertions.

As an example, consider the 2016 Presidential election. It is widely assumed by liberals that sexism drove conservatives to choose Donald Trump, who identifies as a man, over Hillary Clinton, who identifies as a woman. Many held the same view of why some voters chose Bernie Sanders, who ran against Hillary Clinton in the primary election and also identifies as a man, but stopped caring once Clinton won by millions of votes. Compare the differing approaches.

A scholarly approach would quickly dismiss the binary "sexism: yes or no" question as too vague, and seek to define degrees of sexism. Once a rough definition was established, the scholar would need to figure out ways to measure it. Collecting data would likely require applying for a research grant, and polling thousands of people. Then the parsing begins, followed by careful analysis, write up, and debate.

Anyone who does this is stupid.

Much within these tasks is more science than art (read: hard). They are time consuming, and require a rare dedication to the pursuit of knowledge. The process takes so long that the scholar risks the Woke becoming outraged at something entirely different by the time they are ready to present their research (please see "Who is Next?" chapter). And that assumes they reach the correct conclusion!

Far better then to, as white, heterosexual, cisgendered male President George W. Bush used to say, "go with your gut." Obviously there were only two reasons anyone voted for Donald Trump in 2016: sexism, and racism. Anyone arguing otherwise should be mentally placed on probation - maybe they are misguided liberals who will one day Awaken, maybe they are lost souls who will never repent. How they respond to Woke truths will determine which.

To avoid any dreary sojourns into actual scholarship, it is best to rely on the Socratic Method. The Socratic Method relies primarily on discussion and reason to reach conclusions, without all the distracting data. This has two benefits. First, you avoid the more rigorous Scientific Method, which is far more likely to drive you toward objective truth than Woke Truth, and is much more difficult anyway. Second, most people are subconsciously impressed when you invoke Socrates' name. Unless you are addressing a recent law school graduate, most people have long forgotten that what passes for the Socratic Method is often one person with an agenda asking another person leading questions.

The importance of arriving at Woke Truth must not be understated. Data driven models are unreliable, as you can never be sure where you will end up. By largely excluding data and citing other Woke Sophists, you can bypass the messy facts, patterns, and competing explanations that have bogged theorists down for centuries.

Never forget that the answer to scholarly criticism is not strengthening your argument, it is slandering the critic.

Universities

"I don't want you to be safe, ideologically. I don't want you to be safe, emotionally. I want you to be strong. That's different. I'm not going to pave the jungle for you. Put on some boots, and learn how to deal with adversity. I'm not going to take all the weights out of the gym, that's the whole point of the gym."
— *Van Jones (Youtube search: "Van Jones on safe spaces")*

"Education is a method whereby one acquires a higher grade of prejudices."
— *Laurence J. Peter*

Universities are the Woke movement's backbone. It is through universities that We train teachers to push our ideology to students younger than the ones We directly teach on campus. Universities are where We teach undergraduates not how to think, but what to think. By focusing young minds on every horrible thing in American history, ignoring the positives, and viciously attacking anyone as an apologist who favorably compares America's record with other countries', we churn out thousands of angry young activists every year.

But our backbone is under assault. We must mobilize to protect it from the voices of moderation and reason, often in the form of the following complaints.

1. The cost of university education has more than doubled in the last

forty years. (Web search: "nces tuition costs")

2. By stifling unWoke points of view and coercively shoveling endless rounds of assertions down students' throats, the liberal arts have surrendered their claim on teaching critical thinking skills.
3. The majority of our activists are not very useful to employers.

Looking first at costs, the price of a Bachelor's degree has been trending sharply upward since the 1980s. At the same time, middle class wages have flattened. Both of these trends can be laid squarely at the feet of white, heterosexual, cisgendered men. For most Americans, college now means debt, and it is reasonable to ask if that debt is worth taking on when students could enter a trade school, or go directly into a profession that they might end up working in even after receiving a liberal arts degree.

The spike in costs has coincided with the suppression of any criticism of Woke viewpoints, leading moderates to squint at the quality of education their children are receiving for the perpetually inflating tuition. If Woke positions must be shielded from external critique in order to survive, how strong could they be? Are parents and students accepting massive personal debt only to produce activists whose beliefs wither under the barest scrutiny and who are somehow incapable of noticing that?

Which leads us to the final criticism - employers do not need tens of thousands of English majors every year. Increasingly, they need employees with technical skill sets and a positive attitude.

We intend to provide neither.

It is easy to combine the three criticisms of universities in 2020 and wonder if their stunning inability to either adapt to changing needs, or stave off intellectual hijacking by a small group of aggressive people, will necessitate the creation of replacement institutions. Institutions that teach not just vocational training, but the critical thinking skills that are in many cases no longer allowed on college campuses, under pain of ostracization and slander.

On the other hand, it is fully possible that American universities will, over the course of several decades, lose their shine. If another country were to focus more on training students in complex reasoning, and leave the STEM fields in peace, it might begin a slow drain of talent, with international students following.

Both of these possibilities are racist, and fail to consider an unassailable truth - *STEM is hard.* Spending ten minutes reading a single page in a book, only to realize you still do not understand it, is far more taxing than sipping coffee in a small circle and discussing the various failings of other people. We reject the implied hierarchy between people who can do things, and people who can only criticize. As such, not only do We staunchly oppose college majors that lead to careers, as the STEM fields often do, We take an active stance against them under the guise of opposing racism. As shutdownstem.com explains, "Unless you engage directly with eliminating racism, you are perpetuating it."

Moderates may, as implied in the "Silence is Violence" chapter, quickly swap out "racism" for any number of problems, such as "child sex slavery" to demonstrate how utterly unreasonable our demands are, but the current state of liberal arts education ensures they will be immediately set upon by an online mob, not just incapable of using reason and empathy to appreciate the moderate position, but offended by the suggestion of either reason or empathy.

The Media's Role

"Public opinion, in its raw state, gushes out in the immemorial form of the mob's fear. It is piped into central factories, and there it is flavored and colored, and put into cans."
— *H.L. Mencken*

"Journalism is the ability to meet the challenge of filling space."
— *Rebecca West*

Like moderates, the media must by brought to heel. Unlike moderates, this task is largely complete in mainstream organizations such as The New York Times and CNN. Gone are the days when Americans could turn to Fox News for conservative propaganda, MSNBC for liberal propaganda, and have at least some confidence that other traditional outlets were not top-down agenda driven.

This victory must not lull Us into believing the task is concluded. While white, heterosexual, cisgendered male President Trump has been a natural ally to the Woke goal of pushing all traditional media outlets to the radical left, his stated reasons differ, and when he eventually fades from the limelight, more viewers will tune Us out for the less rancorous and absurd world of podcasts.

Perhaps the media's most potent weapon is the amount of ink and air time it dedicates to specific stories. For example, almost no one has heard of Tony Timpa. Timpa was a 32 year old white man who, during a mental health episode, called police on himself, had already been handcuffed by security guards when they arrived, and whose pleas for officers to stop kneeling on his back were caught on film. As Timpa slowly died, officers joked.

Despite a startling similarity to the 2020 George Floyd killing, which sparked not just riots, but nationwide calls to "Defund the Police," Timpa's 2016 killing was barely reported. This was a narrative choice that the Woke movement can continue to enforce with the help of the following chart. Note that anyone presenting this chart as criticism is racist.

Murders Requiring National Coverage

	Asian Killer	Black Killer	LatinX Killer	Native American Killer	White Killer
Asian Victim					
Black Victim					X
LatinX Victim					
Native American Victim					
White Victim					

Critical moderates have argued that while racism obviously exists among any population of humans, the media's knee-jerk leap to racism as the root cause of any killing of a Black person by a white is disingenuous clickbaiting that is, in 2020, actively destabilizing the nation. They wonder if by prioritizing the narrative above data, such as Roland Fryer's 2016 study, "An Empirical Analysis of Racial Differences in Police Use of Force," which found Black people were not shot at higher rates than whites when measured against crimes committed, the media has abandoned its duty to present all relevant facts, as free from bias as human beings can manage.

Indeed, the informed moderate is in a difficult position, as Fryer's study *did* find that Black people were far more likely to have every form of force used against them by police except being shot. Combining Fryer's findings with the media's disinterest in any non-racial violence, and its unwillingness to correct misconceptions such as the Michael Brown's 2014 shooting in Ferguson, Missouri being unjust (after multiple witnesses stated Brown attacked the cop), moderates are left trying to interpret a complicated situation.

The implications, provided one uses the racist tools of logic and reason, are:

1. Racism is definitely a problem that must be addressed.
2. The media is far more interested in activism and sensationalism than providing an accurate picture of any given incident, let alone trends across America.
3. Protesters are protesting the one area of the excessive force spectrum (shootings) where it seems worse to be white, while ignoring everything Fryer identified as truly problematic for Black people (everything except shootings).
4. By shining the brightest spotlight possible on every police shooting (of a Black person), reflexively putting the worst spin on each one, and punishing attempts to find and fix the root cause, the media is practically guaranteeing that Americans will be at each others' throats indefinitely.

Most moderates understand that emotional reactions overwhelm logic, and that policing in America has a long history of oppressing minorities. However their stubborn need for data, accuracy, and continuity retard their Awakening, preventing them from committing to either the radical right or the radical left. Thus they remain vulnerable in much the same way as prisoners with no gang affiliations.

This is where We can use moderates' vacillating need to be factually accurate against them by implying anything less than the full, unquestioning support of everything Woke is equal to bigotry. Use words like "apologist," make casual references to moderates who "went along" with Hitler, and steadfastly refuse to engage them as if they are well-intentioned people who want the best for the Black community while disagreeing with the media's focal points. Becoming exasperated and impatient helps, as does ignoring the possibility that by focusing on symptoms of a deeper problem, the media is dividing the country without actually helping.

Fortunately no one believes they are in a bubble, in the same way no one believes they speak with an accent. They may admit as much when explicitly pressed, but they will forget by the next sentence. This enables anyone, right, left, or center, to criticize their ideological opponents for only considering a narrow, convenient set of facts, while simultaneously doing exactly that. The Woke advantage here is that We may claim that our sources have long-standing histories of quality reporting, while simply neglecting to mention their heartbreaking drop in journalistic integrity.

But We can do more. We must target Hollywood.

I do not mean we must demand more representation for minorities, or that the roles minorities play must be more holistic instead of, for example, constantly casting Arabs as terrorists. Our typical moderate has long accepted these steps as both reasonable and necessary. If the Woke goal was racial harmony, that might suffice (more on that in the "Goals and Solutions" chapter). No, Hollywood must account for its role in the White Supremacist narrative of overcoming adversity.

For a century, Hollywood has created racist propaganda in the form of stories, many of which the unWoke do not recognize as problematic until We lecture them. Take Star Wars. On its face it is a "hero's journey." Young white, heterosexual, cisgendered man Luke Skywalker faces tragedy, and chooses to stand against the nefarious "Empire." Through his struggles, Luke becomes something greater than he was, and saves the galaxy from Darth Vader, a tyrannical Black man.

This is beyond the pale[12]. A young mind simply enjoying a story might not grasp the subtle, racist undertones admonishing them to work hard through adversity, to "pull themselves up by their bootstraps." That the white, heterosexual, cisgendered male Director, George Lucas did not intend the story be interpreted that way is of no relevance in determining his guilt.

A good beginning to Hollywood's atonement came in mid 2020 with the release of a two minute video on Youtube showcasing multiple celebrities repeating, "I take responsibility." These brave multi-millionaires risked everything - from mocking Youtube comments, to mocking Youtube comments - to courageously tell everyone they are against Black people "being slaughtered in the streets." (Web search: "I take responsibility

---

12 I am deeply sorry for any offense I cause by using the phrase "beyond the pale." It may be construed to have some connection with whiteness, but please trust that I would never microaggress my readership like that.

actors")

It is true that moderates are now somewhat wary of many sources We have captured. After years of increasingly Woke narratives leading to events like the noisy resignation of New York Times reporter Bari Weiss, who penned an open letter describing overt bullying of the unWoke (Web search: "Bari Weiss quits"), and NPR's bizarrely promotional interview of an author defending looting, moderates are beginning to wonder if perhaps conservatives had a point all this time. Sure, they say, President Trump may be odious, but does CNN need to spend twenty three hours a day saying so? Is nothing else happening in the world? Did this type of non-stop coverage not contribute to his 2016 election? Are news outlets cynically ginning up outrage over every petty infraction because their business model is threatened?

Similar doubts are creeping into the moderate psyche regarding Hollywood. After a decade of Woke gains, moderates are beginning to wonder if it is perhaps counterproductive to use every platform to deliver an endless stream of Woke lectures, sometimes blatantly addressing the audience by its skin color, and rarely suggesting a realistic, actionable solution.

Fortunately We have a potent weapon on our side - the silent majority's silence.

Your Friend, The Slogan

"I didn't get a harumph out of that guy."
— *Governor Lepetomane*

"Defund the Police" is exactly the heady type of slogan We must continue to propagate.

It is perfect. It is:

1. Succinct. At only three words, its ability to fit on a sticker beats President Trump's "Make America Great Again."
2. Punchy. The phonetics have a natural jab-jab-cross[13] rhythm.
3. Vague. It means different things to different people.

Just as you should never clearly define the terms you use, it is critical to "semantically overload" your slogans - that is, make sure that two reasonable people hearing them can have at least two slightly different interpretations.

In the case of "Defund the Police," it is good and proper to mean police departments should be disbanded, as the police are tools of the racist patriarchy. However, should you be challenged on such a blatantly idiotic suggestion, the deliberate ambiguity of the slogan allows you to claim the more moderate position of merely wanting to shift some portion of tax dollars from unpopular items such as surplus military gear, toward, for

---

13 I apologize to anyone triggered by my microaggression of analogizing Our words to the patriarchal, derelict sport of boxing.

example, addiction counseling.

Moderates often complain that this intentional sleight of hand is divisive, and reminiscent of the "dog whistling" the Woke accuse President Trump of. The key difference between the Woke and Trump is that when We gain power, we will not abuse it - our superior morality will not allow it.

Finally, it is worth pointing out that while the concept of systemic racism states that a system is racist if it produces racist outcomes, even if the participants are not racist, the push to abolish or severely defund police departments is not a form of systemic racism just because it would result in mass chaos and violence in minority communities. In other words, just because following the Woke agenda would get a lot of Black people killed, and the spiking crime rates would drive small businesses away and depress property values for decades, doesn't mean We are now guilty of pushing a systemically racist ideology. If I have to explain why, you would not understand.

Which brings us to the Black Lives Matter (BLM) movement.

As Coleman Hughes, a heterosexual, cisgendered male who happens to be Black, has pointed out, anyone who disagrees with the sentiment that Black lives matter is a monster. Unfortunately he went on to suggest the BLM movement was smuggling additional agenda items into the national discourse under the protection afforded by such an indisputable moral slogan.

BLM's web site is quite clear. From their site: BLM's "mission is to eradicate white supremacy and build local power to intervene in violence inflicted on Black communities by the state and vigilantes."

While that sounds like a sweeping horizon, it is crucial to note that BLM's mission scope is limited to violence perpetrated by external forces. Many have criticized the movement for not caring about the Black lives lost to anyone but white men, typically police officers. In an exchange with actor Terry Crews, CNN's Don Lemon described BLM as, "about police brutality, and injustice in that manner," specifically excluding non-police violence.

Lemon's position is obvious to any non-racist.

Now some point to statements like, "The call for Black lives to matter is a rallying cry for ALL Black lives striving for liberation," found on the BLM web site, as confusing. Some bigots have even wondered why a movement focused on police brutality would not use the word "men" a single time in its six different "About" pages, when young men are the overwhelming victims of police brutality within the Black community. Some wonder why the organization is named "Black Lives Matter" when it explicitly ignores the causes of nearly every Black American's death, or why We get so angry when they are confused by the lack of continuity between what the name implies, and what supporters retreat to it meaning under pressure.

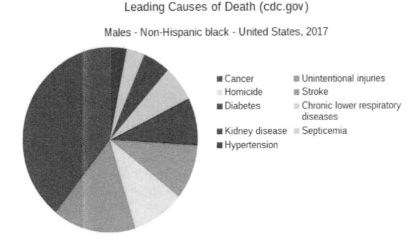

Leading Causes of Death (cdc.gov)

Males - Non-Hispanic black - United States, 2017

The name "Black Lives Matter" was not chosen to ensure that anyone who does not immediately agree with anything We say is labeled a racist, because that would be so cynical and dishonest that moderates would be fools to trust Us with any amount of power.

These questions are irrelevant distractions. What is relevant is that moderates must not be allowed to question the BLM movement. It is not enough for them to vocally agree with the statement that Black lives matter. It is not enough for moderates to support police reform, especially in the form of practical solutions, such as those that heterosexual, cisgendered male and former Presidential contender Andrew Yang has proposed (Web search: "andrew yang police reform"[14]). It is not enough to hesitantly

---

14 From his interview with James Althucher:

1. Have police wear body cameras

support the BLM organization while wondering at the entirety of its goals, as they seem to expand and contract as the situation dictates. It is only good enough when moderates do not merely support the movement, but question anyone who does not agree overtly enough.

Anyone who is confused about the BLM movement is racist.

---

2. Invest in non-lethal weaponry (like bolawrap)

3. Invest in crisis and mental health workers

4. Create a Department of Justice task force around police misconduct to take pressure off of local District Attorneys

5. Demilitarize the police force (they don't need tanks)

Jordan B. Peterson

"For him, 'the left' is anybody to the left of Attila the Hun."
— *Noam Chomsky, 2019 interview for documentary, "Better Left Unsaid"*

"He's really misrepresented, and willfully so. A lot."
— *Joe Rogan, JRE Episode 1141*

Before I begin, please accept my apologies for naming He Who Must Not Be Named. I understand that Jordan B. Peterson (henceforth referred to as "JP" to avoid unnecessarily triggering readers) has, through his violence, and by violence I obviously mean words, harmed millions, and I grieve with you.

With the caveat that he is *literally Hitler*, JP has one major use to the Woke movement - identifying infidels.

JP has thousands of hours of lectures and interviews available any time on Youtube. Anyone with the slightest hint of intellectual curiosity may access them for free to learn what JP thinks and believes. This is not recommended.

All anyone needs to know about JP is he hates transgender people. Now moderates often point out that he has gone out of his way to publicly state on numerous occasions that he does not have a problem with transgender people, will use a person's preferred pronoun if asked to, and was only protesting against a proposed Canadian law that made it illegal to refuse to use preferred pronouns, but this is a deliberate smoke screen. JP has fooled millions of unWoke with his "nuance" and "reason," leading tens of thousands to erroneously state that his books and lectures have helped them become better people, and improve their lives. Many of these unconsciously racist followers claim to agree with JP on some topics, and disagree with him on others, wondering why the Woke cannot do the same rather than misrepresenting him in cartoonish fashion.

As usual we must ignore all counterpoints, lest we learn the wrong lesson. For their own good, the unWoke must be guided through the morass that is JP's intellectual and ethical leanings. For that reason, when someone admits to not knowing much about him, or even who he is, it is your moral obligation to point them to one of dozens of bite-sized hit pieces.

For example, the New York Times has a definitive take down of JP, in which journalist Nellie Bowles notes his "fleeting, suspicious eye contact," a verbal tic he makes that sounds like "a guttural forceful noise," and takes the worst interpretation possible on every facet of JP, ranging from his views on hierarchies to how messy his office is. It is a truly remarkable display of what modern journalism, and the New York Times in particular, has evolved into, and should be required reading.

More useful is Bowles' claim that JP recommends "enforced monogamy," a policy wherein some external actor, presumably the government, forces women to marry undesirable men to stem the latter's violent outbursts.

Critics have pointed out that amid the thousands of hours of video footage of JP detailing his beliefs, he has never so much as hinted at such a stance, and that it contradicts his views on individual freedoms. They ask why he would refrain from voicing that view until he was alone with a New York Times reporter, then deny it, saying that not only does he not believe it, but it is such a stupid idea that no one believes it.

JP's denials insult Us, implying that a reporter for the New York Times would bend facts, or outright manufacture them, in order to push a political agenda. Were he correct, it would indicate that We were actively working to prove accurate his description of the Woke left as some unreasoning nebula, incapable of grasping irony and having whipped itself into a frenzy of resentment and anger.

Some shifty moderates have even opined that by crafting a moral hierarchy with Ourselves above the unWoke, and far superior to the Nazis who support the Republican party, We have made JP's case for the universality of hierarchies in human society. This is offensive, and We must de-platform anyone voicing this opinion until they graduate to a more enlightened stage of thought.

Which brings us back to the previous point. It is imperative We steer the unWoke away from JP's interviews, lectures, and debates - where they might encounter his actual words - and toward the correct interpretation of them.

Edited video clips are a less dangerous alternative, such as the Munk debate on Political Correctness, during which Michael Eric Dyson called JP an "angry white man." (Youtube search: "munk debate angry white man") It is indeed fortunate that only whites can be racist now, or that zinger might have opened Mister Dyson to the charge of racism instead of merely that of derailing an academic debate with an ugly, personal attack deliberately crafted to distract the audience. As it stands, Dyson's performance is a credible representation of the Woke mindset and tactics, and should be viewed by anyone curious about either.

Controlling Language

"If you simplify your English, you are freed from the worst follies of orthodoxy. You cannot speak any of the necessary dialects, and when you make a stupid remark its stupidity will be obvious, even to yourself."
— George Orwell, 'Politics and the English Language,' 1946

Those brave scholars fighting the good fight understand how critical it is to control language. That is why they have focused on re-framing daily life in the most combative terms possible. They are helping build a better society.

For example:

- Students are not "shouting at their professor," they are "speaking truth to power."
- People are not "going about their lives," they are "burying their heads in the sand."
- Other people share "anecdotes," We share "lived experiences."
- "Equality of opportunity" is not a well-intentioned push to provide equal access to resources like textbooks, safe neighborhoods, healthy food, and stable family environments. It is code for "I am racist."
- "Allies" are not people who, despite not suffering from a problem, acknowledge it and want to work with Us to solve it, they are below Us on the Woke Intersectionality hierarchy and subject to any number of fealty tests.
- "Blue lives matter" is a direct assault on Black people, deliberately downplaying Our narrative that all cops are fascists.

The act of repackaging everything in the least favorable manner to enemies of the narrative is required if We are to cow the unWoke into obedience to every stupid idea We have. The merits of each individual point do not matter if we have the ability to scream at critics until they shut up.

This is why, as discussed previously, We re-purposed the word "racist" to describe someone simply living within a system that benefits them. The word already meant something. We could have created or chosen a different word, but that would have robbed Us of the opportunity to attack and shame millions of Americans who grew up agreeing with Martin Luther King Junior.

A fringe benefit of redefining racism is that We can now encourage young Woke acolytes to sever more familial ties. By framing any discomfort with, for example, strict racial quotas in college admissions as evidence of racism, fiery college students will begin to see themselves reflected in social media memes touting the wisdom of cutting "toxic" people from their lives. Isolating young adults from their support network is but another step in making sure the only ideas they hear are Ours, and if they hear any facts, those facts reinforce Us.

We can do more.

For example, many of the protests following the 2020 killing of George Floyd have included some rioting and some looting. It is insufficient for moderate liberals to acknowledge that most protesters are peaceful and that police brutality is a problem that needs to be addressed, particularly in regards to Black Americans. It is insufficient for moderate liberals to support legislation addressing police brutality. What is required is an explicit statement that:

1. All Cops Are Bastards (ACAB), and part of the problem.
2. Rioting and looting are justified.
3. Burning down a building only *seems* violent.

We must conflate the terms "rioting" and "looting" with racist dog whistles, ignoring the fact that many of the rioters and looters are white Woke people, and many of the victims are minorities. The movement must not slow down for such petty nuance.

Next, the word "Antifa," short for "anti-fascist," is sacrosanct. Many a moderate has complained that pulling fire alarms at lectures you dislike, or hitting people for saying things you disagree with is actually quite fascistic. These views must be silenced, or Our anti-fascism work will never progress to enforcing social harmony. Moderates must understand that, in the same way the Chinese People's Liberation Army exists, by definition, to liberate people, anything Antifa does is, by definition, fighting fascism.

Finally, the word "problematic" deserves special recognition. Of every weapon in the outrage arsenal, "problematic" is perhaps the most subtle. It is the perfect dog whistle - vague enough to permit retreat when pressed, but well enough understood to ferret out troublemakers. Anyone familiar enough with methods of authoritarian population control to shudder at the implications of labeling a thought "problematic" will implicitly understand the threat and remain quiet.

Repeated use of "problematic" is the mark of someone who can smile while painting a target on another person's back.

Some moderates have scoffed at the notion that words are violence, in part because those making the claim tend to say incredibly offensive things like "all men are trash," but also because they can smell another blank check. When juxtaposed against the claim that rioting is acceptable, the Woke look patently absurd. We must discourage people from discussing how words are violence, as they eventually arrive at the familiar claim of subjectivity. It is possible to absolutely crush a person by saying something monstrous, such as using racial slurs that dehumanize them. It is also possible to weaponize the sympathy inherent in most moderate people by claiming aggrieved status at the slightest disagreement.

It is the Woke's duty to exploit moderates' sympathy to shut down any push back on our ideas, lest those ideas be forced to stand or fall on their own merit.

Intersectionality Jenga

"Straightforwardness and simplicity are in keeping with goodness."
— Seneca

The essence of intersectionality is to reject the holistic view of any human being, and replace it with one or more dominant, oppressed characteristics. There is some latitude for a person to choose their defining characteristic - after all we are not fascists - but it must come from an oppressed class. For example, if a person is a transgender, Jewish, Asian woman, she may choose either transgender or woman. This is not to imply there is a difference between men and women, or that only two biological sexes exist. Please do not cancel me. Not that Cancel Culture exists.

Some moderates have opined that intersectionality is a house of cards that artificially lumps disparate groups together solely by virtue of a common enemy - the white, cisgendered, heterosexual male. As the Woke movement provides no counterpoint more coherent than plugging its ears and shouting, "LALALA I CAN'T HEAR YOU," moderates incorrectly surmise that the intersectional foundation of the Woke movement is already cracking, and that the movement is bound to fall apart in spectacular fashion, having accomplished very little in the way of civil rights progress while leaving mistrust, destruction, and racial discord in its wake.

Obviously this is nonsense. Gay men and transsexuals, for example, have plenty in common, despite what they say, as do Black men and lesbians. Their most important similarity is they all must define themselves first and foremost by the trait most traditionally oppressed by white, heterosexual, cisgendered males. If one is a gay lawyer and father of two who enjoys golf, they are, for Our purposes, simply gay.

Intersectionality has uncovered bigotry in surprising places, such as the persistent derision bisexuals report from the gay community. The most egregious offender, however, is the Trans-Exclusionary Radical Feminist (TERF). TERFs hold to the outdated premise that there is a difference between men and women, pitting them squarely against the 27 trans activists that dictate how all of America may discuss the bevy of new issues confusing the country. These TERFs insist on "protecting women," as if women are somehow different than men, and are loath to permit "biological men" into "female spaces" such as women's locker rooms, battered women's shelters, women's sports, or women's prisons.

There is impressively little data on how introducing trans women into these spaces will affect them, and We mean to keep it that way because We already know the answers - trans women are women, period. Any distinction is transphobic, as is any attempt to study the topic. For further admonitions against study, see the "Scholarship" chapter.

The prohibition against study must be extended to include intersectionality as a whole. Not by Woke scholars of course, but by anyone capable of reaching the wrong conclusion. For example, if a well-intentioned government body commissioned a study on intersectionality for the purposes of crafting legislation to actually solve problems rather than bitch incessantly about them, that study would have to be conducted by Woke scholars. Otherwise the results could indicate that although the concept of intersectionality - the idea that a single individual can face simultaneous bigotry for being a woman, a Black person, and gay - is both demonstrable and concerning, there is no workable Woke solution to be had beyond pelting Americans with advertisements.

Traitors To The Cause

"By the logic of gay liberation, Thiel is an example of a man who has sex with other men, but not a gay man."
— Jim Downs, author of Stand By Me: The Forgotten History of Gay Liberation (Citation from: The Advocate, "Peter Thiel Shows Us There's a Difference Between Gay Sex and Gay")

"I had to remind him that he was a black person, so he can't vote for Donald Trump."
— Chelsea Handler

Woke activists are amazing people who suffer the slings and arrows[15] of outrageous bigotry on Our behalf. Not content to prosecute "classical" racism, Our Inquisitors happily sniff out the slightest indication of implicit bias. The mark of the beast may take many forms, including:

- Mixing up two actors, or forgetting one's name (unless the actor(s) is white).
- Flinching at non-heteronormative public displays of affection (PDA). Flinching at heterosexual PDAs is permitted, provided both participants are white, though in many cases this may be seen as "slut shaming," as the flincher is always offended by the woman's

---

15 I am *so sorry* for referencing Shakespeare while so many women, men, and other Americans are yet heinously oppressed by the legacy of Anglo/Saxon conquest.

actions and not the man's.
- Taking more than one day to signal support for a Woke cause on social media.

Some moderates claim Woke activists do not speak for the communities they purport to represent simply because those communities did not "choose" them, and members are "individuals" with different "views." These moderates often claim that it is, in fact, racist for Us to treat minority communities as monolithic blocks that will fall in line behind whatever agenda we push on their behalf, no matter how infantilizing it may be.

Obviously these moderates must be dealt with immediately using every weapon in the Woke arsenal, which usually translates into slandering the speaker as a bigot. But what do We do with the oppressed who do not think they are oppressed?

Here We must turn to Morpheus:

"The Matrix is a system, Neo. That system is our enemy. But when you're inside, you look around, what do you see? Businessmen, teachers, lawyers, carpenters. The very minds of the people we are trying to save. But until we do, these people are still a part of that system and that makes them our enemy. You have to understand, most of these people are not ready to be unplugged. And many of them are so inert, so hopelessly dependent on the system that they will fight to protect it."

As such, Black Americans may slur fellow Black Americans as "Uncle Toms" when they stray from Woke Truth. Some apostates push back, unreasonably pointing out that this de-platforms good people who have thought through their positions and deserve the basic respect of being heard before they are personally attacked to avoid engaging them on ideas or beliefs.

Setting aside that racist appeal to logic, what matters is these apostates' hurtful refusal to accept the critique that, by holding conservative values, they are not acting Black. Do not confuse this with Vice President Joe Biden's admonition that Black Americans either vote for him or "they ain't black." That was racist, and Biden clearly had not read my chapter, "Talking About Race."

A better example is Cheryl Dorsey, a Black, retired police officer who disagreed with Kentucky Attorney General Daniel Cameron's decision to not bring charges against the cop who shot and killed Breonna Taylor. In an MSNBC interview, Dorsey says of Cameron, "He's 'skin folk,' but he is not 'kin folk.'" This is an acceptable way to tell someone to act their color. While puzzled moderates may wonder what Cameron should have charged the officers with, as they only began shooting after Taylor's boyfriend opened fire on them while they were serving a warrant, We must resist the temptation to allow racist propaganda like facts or the law to muddy the narrative. Clearly this is a case of racist cops gunning down Black people without repercussion. If the top prosecutor in the state is Black, that does not disprove our assertion of universal racism, it merely proves that the country needs the Woke to shout louder. Fortunately we have entire media outlets dedicated to the suppression of inconvenient facts.

Allowing Black liberals to chastise Black conservatives for not acting how they ought to, based on skin color, does not imply that white liberals can tell white conservatives (or vice versa) to act their color. That is racist. The only acceptable way to tell white people to act their own color is via cultural appropriation.

Cultural appropriation is not, as some well meaning unWoke have argued, a problem wherein white people mischaracterize other cultures, or exploit them for profit. Instead it is a matter of white people being annoying. They have rock and roll, yet they must enjoy rap. They have straight hair, yet they must fashion it into dread locks. This is not youthful emulation of a culture young whites admire, it is oppression.

But whites are not the only ones who can be lambasted to stay in their racial lane. In 2017, NBA star Kenyon Martin bravely confronted fellow NBA star Jeremy Lin, via online comments, for the Asian star's dread locks, saying, among other things, "Come on man, somebody need to tell him, like, 'all right bro, we get it. You wanna be black.' Like, we get it. But your last name is Lin."

While Martin's comments may sound racist on their face, they are not. Because Martin is not white. On the other hand, Lin's seemingly conciliatory response - wishing the African American community admiration and respect while pointing out that Martin had Chinese writing tattooed on his arm - was a truly abhorrent moment in sports.

Cultural appropriation is another area that confuses thoughtful moderates, who point out that Black people have long complained that whites look down on their culture, including the way they dress, speak, sing, or gesture. Yet when confronted by white teenagers who so admire Black culture that they attempt to emulate it, Woke activists call them racist as well. The rules whites must follow regarding any[16] other culture are as simple as the ones they must follow when discussing race (see my "Talking About Race" chapter).

1. Do not criticize other cultures.
2. Do not emulate other cultures.
3. Do not make assumptions about other cultures.
4. Learn about other cultures.
5. Do not make others feel they must be "ambassadors" by asking questions about their culture.
6. Notice and appreciate the differences between cultures.
7. Compliment other cultures, but only in ways that will not annoy or offend.
8. Do not make others feel awkward by fawning over their culture.
9. Avoid profiting from another culture by, for example, serving Mexican food. Only serve traditionally white food.

By following these simple steps, which may grow at any given moment, whites can help usher in a level of interracial comfort heretofore unknown in America.

---

16 While the Woke generally ignore Asian people, for the purposes of chastising white teenagers who would like to wear Geisha dresses, We will make an exception. While no one in Japan could care less, that just means Japanese people need Us more, because if a group will not get offended, We must do so on its behalf.

Silence Is Violence

"There is only one way to happiness and that is to cease worrying about things which are beyond the power of our will."
— *Epictetus*

Because America is a white supremacist country, anyone who does not loudly repeat various anti-racist slogans is committing violence upon all minorities. This is not psychological manipulation.

Whites, in particular the cisgendered, heterosexual men, are notoriously guilty of tacitly invoking their privilege with phrases like, "There's an alarming discrepancy between how much force police officers use on Black and white suspects, but abolishing police departments sounds like it will get a lot of minorities killed."

Being open to a multitude of sensible solutions to a well-defined problem is no defense. Agreeing that a problem exists, while arguing that it is complicated, and needs a complicated set of solutions, is despicable.

But We are not here to talk about solutions, We are here to remind America that collectivized guilt requires collectivized atonement. We are watching. We see who is not standing up for justice. We. Will. Remember.

Some of the unWoke wonder how they can stand against racial injustice when they end each day tired and anxious. Many barely cover living expenses, have no emergency money, lousy or no health insurance, children to watch and teach since the Covid19 pandemic has closed schools, and various other demands on their life. The Truth is often difficult to hear, but if they cared, they would find a way.

This is no time for empathy.

Other unWoke question the logic (a sign of racism) behind "Silence is Violence," pointing out that there are any number of atrocities happening throughout the world that have equal claim to their time and energy. Problems like:

1. A million Uighur Muslims in Chinese concentration camps. (Web search: "chinese concentration camps")
2. Over 5.6 million Syrian refugees as of September 2020, more than half of whom are children. (Web search: "syrian refugees today")
3. Covid19, also known as "the Corona virus," killing, as of this writing, roughly 1,000 Americans a day, forcing millions into economic uncertainty, isolation, and destabilizing mental health worldwide. (Web search: … anything, really)
4. Sex trafficking, often involving children. (Do not search for this)

Given these, and uncounted other problems, they ask, how is it reasonable to condemn a person who agrees with your basic premise but is too overwhelmed by the magnitude of life, especially during 2020's Covid19 lockdowns, to keep up?

If we were reasonable We would not be Woke, and these moderates can stuff their privileged expectations.

Moderates that subscribe to various spiritual belief systems are inherently at odds with Our demand that they become angry about the exact injustice We point at, the moment We point at it. Christians have the Serenity Prayer, for example, while studious atheists may look to Stoics like Epictetus, ancient bastion of white male privilege that he was. What they do not realize is Woke scholars, through rigorous agreement with each other and relentless slandering of all critics, have supplanted previous sources of wisdom.

Finally, a thoughtful moderate may notice the moral judgment implicit in the phrase, "Silence is Violence." Someone, often who knows nearly nothing about them, is telling them that the way they are living their life is morally unacceptable. This someone is simultaneously informing them of a problem they did not know they had, while offering them the remedy, and instead of being grateful for the guidance, the typical, fragile response is to become offended.

Where We Go From Here

"America Must Be Destroyed"
— Gwar

At this point you are probably wondering how you can best help the Woke Movement. This section provides a set of steps a transcendent individual may take.

Goals And Solutions

Seagull Management:
The seagull manager flies in, makes a lot of noise, craps on everything then
flies off again leaving a big mess behind
— Urban Dictionary

It is not the job of the Woke Movement to provide solutions to the problems It identifies. These problems existed long before Us.

Racism is an obvious example. A common criticism of Woke ideology is that there is no "there" there. Once the unWoke understand how impure they are, there is no next step. No cleansing ritual, no forgiveness, just a sort of stewing in one's own rot.

This is not true. While the Woke Movement may not have an articulate destination, it is imperative that We tear down the racist, sexist, ableist, cis/heteronormative[17] structures that imprison modern Americans, almost always without their awareness.

What, moderates often ask, do the Woke plan to build to replace today's hellscape of oppression after We finish burning every institution and cultural norm to the ground? We have no idea. Or we are not going to tell them. We have not decided yet. It does not matter.

The stubborn moderate often clings to this point, saying things like, "You would not quit the job you dislike before having another job." This

---

17 List of intersectionally oppressed subject to change.

statement is so incredibly privileged it boggles the mind. Others point out how angry We were when President Trump tried to dismantle the Affordable Care Act, aka "Obamacare," without a ready replacement. How We rightly concluded that simply destroying an imperfect solution without offering a comparable one sounded like it would have made millions of people's lives worse.

Any comparison between the Woke attempt to tear down all American norms and institutions without enunciating what comes after the destruction, and President Trump's attempt to do exactly that with Obamacare is unfair. We reject it as racist and hurtful.

The most obscene criticism that moderates level at the Woke movement is that there is no reason to believe, given Our current behavior, that We would re-make society into anything a sane[18] person would want to live in. This argument betrays the speaker's ignorance of the CHAZ experiment.

CHAZ, short for Capitol Hill Autonomous Zone, (which changed its name to CHOP - Capitol Hill Organized Protest) was a six block, "police-free" area of Seattle that lasted nearly a month. Some moderates have heard of CHAZ, but fail to see the progress it achieved. Instead they point to minor issues like:

- Within days of declaring the CHAZ takeover, occupants erected borders, with armed guards challenging people wishing to enter.
- To maintain safety, CHAZ recreated the Seattle Police Department (SPD) via armed men patrolling the area, only now the armed men policing CHAZ had undergone no background checks, were accountable to no one, and allowed a massive increase in crime to happen.
- Homeless people quickly stole all their food, leading to CHAZ residents to ask for donations. (Web search: "chaz homeless stole food").
- Emergency services such as paramedics were deliberately impeded.

Allowing the Woke to run a micro-city for a month, they argue, resulted in utter chaos, including:

---

18 Please accept my most sincere regrets at using the word "sane." I understand the hurt that word can cause to people struggling with mental health issues, and wanted to leave it out, but felt it accurately depicted the anti-sensitivity of today's moderate liberal.

"An increase of 525%, 22 additional incidents, in person-related crime in the area, to include two additional homicides, 6 additional robberies, and 16 additional aggravated assaults (to include 2 additional non-fatal shootings) between June 2nd and June 30th, 2020, compared to the same period of time in 2019" (Web search: "seattle Executive Order 2020-08")

Again, We must point out that it is not our job to create a safe and/or prosperous replacement for the white supremacist America of today. It is only our job to tear it down.

This especially applies to Police Departments (PDs) across the country. Sure, CHAZ may have demonstrated how lethal abolishing PDs will be, and how ineffectual the communal replacements are. And yes, We may sound like children playing at being adults, but that is a risk We are willing to take.

Black community leaders may not be willing to take that risk with Us, as they often have to live in the areas we want to de-police. The mayor of Newark, New Jersey, for example, called efforts to Defund The Police a "bourgeois liberal" solution, perhaps in reference to the fact that so many of the protesters are white and do not live in the high crime areas that would benefit from Our ideas.

Many of Us may not be Black, We may not live in the areas that would be most affected by a diminished police presence, and yes, We probably do not shop or visit these places, or even know anyone who does, but that does not mean We do not know what is best for those communities.

The last peril we face is the idea that We should join our local police force. The malformed logic behind this suggestion is that the Woke would solve the problem of police brutality by bringing to bear Our innate moral loftiness. Either that or We would gain first-hand knowledge and experience in law enforcement, knocking Us off Our pedestal as We tried, and failed, to do a better job.

Taking definitive action to solve a problem is hard, and we will not be coerced into doing it. Furthermore We are offended by the implied criticism that the Woke are too busy criticizing people doing things to take action ourselves. By pointing out, even accidentally, that the Woke are most interested in positions such as journalist, politician, or Human Resources officer, where We tell everyone else how to do the work, moderates betray their sympathy for the racist ideal of "doing things."

Finally, We will not tolerate anything that might lead to empathy with the enemy, or dull Our resolve to tear it all down.

Who Is Next

"Great persecutors are recruited among martyrs whose heads haven't been cut off."
— Emil Cioran

"I didn't even know we was after Saddam Hussein, I thought we was after bin Laden, what happened? ... When did bin Laden give Hussein the baton of hate? When did he pass it on? Like 'they hate me, they hate me, they hate me ... they hate you! Run!'"
— Chris Rock

A common criticism of the Woke movement is it is exhausting. Nearly every day We are launching a campaign of some sort, mobbing someone on Twitter for a relatively minor infraction, or at the very least trying Our best to drum up outrage. While true, this critique both comes from a place of straight, white, cisgendered, ableist, monogamous, male privilege (or internalized misogyny/racism/heteronormality if the provocateur is not a straight, white, cisgendered, et cetera, male), and ignores the larger pattern.

Since the mid-2010s, the Woke movement has focused Our Eye of Sauron on specific groups in turn.

The Woke "baton of hate" progression.

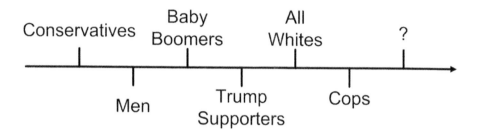

While We have definitely maintained a jaw-dropping level of outrage week on week for years, often conflating corner cases with trends, We have reserved Our focused efforts for the irredeemable characteristics shown above.

It is tempting to view this steady march of anger and think, "this encompasses most of the country. How can a movement hate most of the country?" Quite easily, it turns out, provided one studiously avoids befriending or engaging anyone from the unclean group.

Individual action is no way to mitigate one's association with any of these groups, but one can combine an unfavorable group association with a favorable one. It is complicated, but as the baton of hate passes from one group to another, an Oppressor may find themselves Oppressed. Given the right mood on Twitter, this may override Oppressor status. For example men, many of whom were surprised to find out they were all garbage during the #metoo movement, (Web search: "yes all men") may also be transgender, Muslim, or Black. In this case the Woke movement will grant them a reprieve, based on the momentary needs of the narrative.

A concrete example occurred in August of 2020, a white cop was filmed shooting a Black man, Jacob Blake, in the back seven times while getting into a car with his kids inside. The normal response to this is anger, outrage, grief, even resignation, followed by confusion as a second video surfaced showing Blake fighting with police, and more details emerged. Details such as the police being on scene at the behest of Blake's girlfriend, Blake having a knife on the seat of the car he was getting into, and having an outstanding arrest warrant for domestic abuse and third degree sexual assault, defined as:

- *Sexual intercourse with a person without consent of that person, or*
- *Sexual contact with intentional penile ejaculation with a person without consent of that person.*

(Web search: "definitions and wisconsin laws")

At this point, most moderates hesitate to lionize Blake, presumably because "Sexual intercourse with a person without consent of that person" sounds a lot like rape, and they have been repeatedly told to "believe all women" in regards to rape allegations. When the incident is viewed in its entirety instead of through the Woke prism of "everything is racist," the average moderate grows silent. Fortunately Vice President Kamala Harris is Woke, and therefore unconstrained by the need to know if an alleged rapist is guilty before telling him she is "proud of him."

Harris is such a warrior that when a Supreme Court Justice nominee was accused of sexual assault more than 30 years prior, she tweeted, "Wore black today in support of all survivors of sexual assault or abuse. We won't let them be silenced or ignored. #BelieveSurvivors." It is not Vice President Harris' fault that the Woke movement's anger, attention, and empathy all have a shelf life dictated by convenience. She is the leader the Woke movement deserves.

Given the complicated circumstances of the case, many moderates wonder if society should wait to find out more. They say the cop in question may still be guilty, but the matter seems to warrant "investigation" (code for "I am a racist"). They want to know more about the knife, for example, before deciding if the cop should be prosecuted, and are uninterested in hearing the phrase "in front of his kids" repeated ad nauseum.

Any reservations about Blake's tragic circumstances and heroism is openly racist. Any criticism of Harris' perceived insincerity is a distraction. Any hesitation to rightly label the entire incident a clear example of racism should result in the demonization of the moderate as alt-right, and, if We can uncover their employer's name, lead to their being fired.

More importantly, the Blake tragedy contradicts the characterization of the Woke movement as astonishingly unforgiving, illustrating its ability to overlook transgressions, such as being male, or an accused rapist, when they are counterbalanced by a person's usefulness to the Woke narrative. Still, the question remains: Who is next to bear the baton of hate?

The answer, of course, is We have no idea.

All Your Culture Are Belong To Us

"Criticism is a study by which men grow important and formidable at very small expense."
— Samuel Johnson

"WARNING: The inside fold out to this record cover is a work of art by H.R. Giger that some people may find shocking, repulsive or offensive. Life can sometimes be that way."
— Warning label on Dead Kennedies album

Like your helpful friend who recently discovered nutrition and provides endless, unrequested insight into your lunch choices, the Woke are an essential cultural guide. No one else is equipped to list everything problematic with every piece of art, be it movie, book, or song. No one else has the time, energy, or interest to systematically cancel everything created before 1970[19].

Bigoted critics often claim this quality makes Woke people about as likable, and useful, as a car alarm. Misguided moderates argue they *know* people who lived decades or centuries ago all held beliefs deemed unacceptable in 2020. They seem to feel that retroactively applying modern standards to people long dead is unreasonable, and a waste of time, preferring to admire certain qualities in a person while acknowledging or condemning other qualities, then moving on with their lives.

---

19 Exceptions may be granted based on Our collective love of Disneyland.

Moderates are typically conflicted on issues like tearing down statues, shrugging at the loss of more egregious characters like Confederate leaders, but wondering, when We turn to George Washington, how to balance the good and evil done by someone who lived centuries ago. This equivocating, often spun as "thinking," or "debating," may be Hitlerian in nature, but it is to Our benefit. While moderates hem and haw, We of a singular focus may act. Our only impediment is conservatives, including moderates We push toward conservatism.

The truly reprehensible ask if We, the Woke of 2020, would like to be judged by mobs of arrogant 20-somethings fifty years from now. They suggest We are doing things that future Woke will find morally unforgivable, perhaps to the point that Our names will be cursed. This is preposterous, as We are not a product of Our times, We are Woke.

Comedians are another matter. Many comics are basically intellectuals with massive childhood trauma, combining a lack of impulse control with the same insightfulness that makes intellectuals difficult to trick. This, unfortunately, means comics tend to be braver than intellectuals, or at least less careful, and are thus harder to control.

Their growing backlash against Woke "overreach" is concerning. As recently as 2010 it was difficult to find any comedian willing to criticize Us. The list was short, and easily hissed at:

1. Dennis Miller
2. Nick DiPaolo

By 2020, the list of Nazis had grown to include[20]:

1. Joe Rogan
2. Andrew Shultz
3. Jerry Seinfeld
4. Dave Chappelle
5. Jim Jeffries
6. Bridget Phetasy
7. Bill Maher

This is not to say those on the 2020 list hold many conservative views. In fact the views of those miscreants are overwhelmingly left-leaning. But that is not enough. Jim Jeffries, for example, hosts a show espousing many liberal ideas and values, but he criticized Us in a Netflix special, and that intolerance must be punished.

Moderates often wonder if so many mainstream comics criticizing the Woke movement is perhaps a sign We have gone too far. That perhaps We are a bunch of censorious, overgrown babies who crumble at the slightest emotional touch, and while some of our aims are laudable, We need to be reined in by actual adults. Perhaps, they wonder, if Our stance that laughing at any misfortune constitutes "punching down," the Woke are declaring that nothing is funny, and are ruining comedy for everybody.

This is not accurate, as We have a generous list of precisely who and what comedians are permitted to mock or mention. Thus if Cancel Culture existed, it would be for anyone holding these libertine, pro-comic views.

---

20 While there are undoubtedly more stubbornly disobedient comics, those who are less established are vulnerable enough to know their place and stick to approved art.

21st Century Policing

"John Lewis and I were very concerned when these slogans came out about 'defund the police.' We sat together on the House floor and talked about how that slogan... could undermine the BLM movement, just as 'burn, baby, burn' destroyed our movement back in the '60s."

— *Jim Clyburn (D) South Carolina*

All Cops Are Bastards (ACAB).

As We tend to be the most enlightened people in any given room, it is incumbent upon Us to explain how we may vilify an entire group of people for vilifying an entire group of people. To most moderates, this seems as nakedly hypocritical as opposing protests We disagree with during the Covid19 pandemic because the protesters would spread the disease, then, weeks later, supporting protests we agree with. Let me assure you that nothing is as nakedly hypocritical as that.

The key difference between Black people and cops is that cops chose to be cops, and can choose to stop being cops. Being a cop is neither immutable, nor an accident of birth, and anyone caught vilifying a person for something they neither chose, nor can change about themselves, is a foul human being.

Any moderate of average reasoning might still ask how We could attack tens of thousands of cops, many of whom are People of Color and/or women, when We know nothing about them (Youtube search: "white woman yells at black cop", Youtube search: "black portland police officer jackson"). The answer is simple: We know enough.

Cops are not complicated individuals driven by different motivations, with childhoods, emotions, dreams, struggles, failings, and strengths. They are a uni dimensional entity in a uniform. A tool of white supremacy. This dehumanization process allows Us to eschew all nuance as we re-make policing. For example, any reporter or Twitter user can tell you that it is racist to discuss a suspect's past, or behavior leading up to a violent incident[21], but the cop's history must be publicly scrutinized. We will not hold Ourselves to the same standard as them for the same reason We refuse to circulate unedited videos - nuance confuses people.

That is why courts of law continue to let Hitler after Hitler go free when the court of public opinion has long condemned them. By forcing people to sit quietly and absorb all relevant facts instead of the ones We cherry pick, our racist courts guarantee juries reach a different conclusion than angry people on Facebook who have dedicated up to twenty minutes reading articles on any given incident. We must tear it down.

Future policing will be voluntary, and far more gentle. Cops, the few professional ones that persist, will be told to avoid violence at all costs.

A common critique from moderates is that We are asking for empathy, for people to envision "walking a mile in Our shoes," while angrily refusing cops the same courtesy. The more abrasive moderates ask why no Woke critics have become cops, since We are so convinced We could do a better job. Why not stop criticizing for once and actually do something, they ask.

We are doing something. By tirelessly criticizing police, then scampering away when asked to do the job Ourselves, We are bringing about the end of white supremacy. By dumping on police instead of encouraging Our young activists to be the change they want to see in the world, we are using the time-honored Republican approach of demonizing and, hopefully, under funding a government agency we despise, so We may one day point to its poor performance.

Critics wonder if, by vilifying all cops, We are driving good cops to other

---

21 Recall from the chapter on the media that for an incident to be worth reporting, the suspect must be Black. It would not be racist to delve into, for example, a white or Asian suspect's behavior or history, but there is no reason for those incidents to be reported.

careers while making future applicant pools smaller. This, they argue, will lead to less effective policing, higher crime rates in low income areas, and perhaps even more excessive force problems as police departments have to accept candidates they previously would have rejected.

While these are definite possibilities, it is racist to point them out. Just as it is racist to wonder if richer areas will hire private police forces, leading to walled-off neighborhoods with fully staffed, private police departments, while poor areas remain chronically under policed and dangerous.

One might ask how any of this is helpful, how anything We are doing is alleviating the measurable difference between how Black and white men are treated during routine encounters with law enforcement. Could the frequency of those encounters indicate a deeper problem, of which police violence is a symptom? Are We failing to separate good from bad cops because We are intellectually lazy? Do good cops fail to report or stand up to bad cops because of the same pressures that cause peaceful protesters to watch looters and rioters ruin their demonstration? Are We just making things worse?

No.

The future of policing in America is as benevolent as it is Woke.

Hire Woke!

"We don't know what we want, but we are ready to bite somebody to get it."
— *Will Rogers*

As the chapter name implies, the most effective way to build a brighter future is to always hire Woke.

This is not just about helping society. Think of all the benefits your team, office, or company can reap from dropping just one Woke person into the current environment.

1. After 1-2 scoldings, insensitive jokes will stop. After another 1-2 scoldings, all jokes will, leading to a more professional team.
2. As coworkers understand the danger of casual banter, they will instinctively stay quiet. Imagine the productivity gains your team will realize as people re purpose the time they used to spend getting to know one another with direct, focused replies.
3. Human Resources will have its very own political officer embedded within various divisions of the company.
4. With a culture of fear and mistrust in place, employees will feel obligated to work harder, and ask for fewer raises or perks.
5. Any rabblerousers will leave, or, if they are stubborn, stay, but provide the Woke —> Human Resources pipeline with a dossier filled with microaggressions.
6. You will never need to worry if there is any subtle racism, sexism,

or any other form of bigotry "flying under the radar,"[22] because your Woke employees will noisily inform you of problematic views, often via posts to social media sites like Twitter.

7. Policing your own actions will no longer be a concern, since the moment you fail to act on any complaints, your Woke employees will contact your boss.

The trickiest part of hiring Woke is identifying Us, however there is a handy shortcut. While asking job candidates about their political beliefs is "illegal," the following approaches are not:

1. Inquire about their majors in college. If systemic oppression kept them from university life, ask what majors interested them the most.
2. Search their social media postings with an eye toward Cancelling people. Obviously this does not prove the existence of Cancel Culture, but if the candidate has shown repeated enthusiasm for wrecking the lives of people who disagree with their politics, you have a catch on your hands!
3. Ask them to solve 2 + 2 (Web search: "woke 2+2"). If they answer with a quizzical cock of the head and the number 4, they are tools of the western patriarchy.

Utilizing the above tactics will more often than not result in successfully identifying the Woke, though it is hard to be more specific because I do not believe in statistics.

Some moderates wonder if spending hours per week in a quasi-meditative hunt for their own bigotry is a productive way to work. Pointing to complaints by people who used to get along well with coworkers, but after Diversity training feel awkward, and no longer part of the same team, they ask if we will soon see employees quitting to start their own companies. Companies that will ignore Woke ideologues, focus on getting work done, and entice top performers to join them. Companies that will be in a position to crush their former employers.

This racist compartmentalization will never materialize, as Woke workers

---

22 My sincerest apologies for invoking military symbolism. I understand that all airplanes can be used for evil and are thus tools of white supremacy. I chose to use this uncomfortable term based on the many humanitarian missions I have read about that utilized aircraft. Please forgive any triggering on my part.

are the top performers. They consistently out-Tweet the unWoke, and are often the only workers in an entire cubicle farm with visible political stickers.

Companies must fully internalize that while capitulating to Woke demands will never appease Us, they must do so nonetheless. Imagine your office as a still pond. Imagine the ripples caused by dropping a pebble into that pond. Notice how they emanate outward in all directions from a single point, reaching farther than you ever expected. Now replace the pebble with a giant rock, and heave it into the pond of your office.

You are welcome.

The Language Of Future Catastrophes

"You know, the Nazis had pieces of flair that they made the Jews wear."
— *Peter Gibbons*

It is reasonable to wonder how We might distinguish between normal racists - meaning all whites - and the more classical racist. This is not to suggest that whites are ever morally acceptable, just that most do not justify the same degree of fear and hatred as neo-Nazis, or members of the Aryan Nation.

The challenge we face is linguistic. By painting tens of millions of Americans with the worst smear possible save "pedophile," we have nothing left to call them when they actually do racist things. Moreover, since racism is undeniably grotesque, and all whites are racist, one could justify walking up to the nearest white and punching them in the face (which, for legal purposes, I urge readers not to do). We may indeed change the definition of "pedophile" in the future to describe what the word "racist" used to, but for now I recommend the "+" designation for its inherent scalability. Please see the following chart for clarification.

Racist categories for whites

Term	Characteristics
Racist	White skin. Cutoff point flexible.
Racist+	White that will not admit they are racist.
Racist++	White that unnecessarily describes skin color. For example, "my Mexican coworker and I are having dinner together tonight."
Racist+++	White that uses the phrase "black on black crime."
Racist++++	…

By using a numerical system, We can add as many rules and classifications as we want until it becomes impossible for anyone to get along. This also empowers Us with a verbal shorthand. Rather than "He is a racist plus plus plus," We may slander strangers with the abbreviated, "He is a racist-three-plus," or, if one prefers, "He is a three-plus-racist." This may even be winnowed down to "He is a three plus," or, "He's a three." The system allows a fair degree of customization, and lets Woke scholars debate (with each other, of course) when a white's racism warrants violence. Finally, it gives whites a goal - they may, through years of awkward self flagellation, work their way down the chart to the point of being merely racist.

Eventually, a Woke person calling a white "racist" will be considered a compliment, as it means the white has refrained from (or hidden …) any of the problematic views or actions that would necessitate them being reclassified as "racist+" or worse.

However racism is not the only area in which the Woke movement has catastrophized itself into a linguistic corner. "Transphobe," in theory, describes someone who fears, or perhaps hates, transgender people. In practice it is hurled at many a wide-eyed onlooker who could not care less what is happening in some stranger's pants, but is utterly baffled by all the new rules. These misguided moderates believe they have the right to ask questions like:

1. "My daughter came home one day and announced she is a boy. I support trans rights but she never showed any signs of gender confusion before her friend transitioned. What do I do?"

2. "Isn't it a little unfair that male athletes can transition at 30 years old and crush biological female athletes?"

Questioners may hide behind a desire to have genuine conversations in which trans points are given thoughtful consideration alongside cisgendered ones, but their intent is of no import. A hunt for fair and equitable answers to difficult problems is no excuse for asking uncomfortable questions, and, however well intentioned these moderates may be, a Twitter mob must hound them until they repent.

The "plus" system has merit here as well. There are subtle differences between, for example, a sympathetic but confused moderate, and someone who wants all trans people to die. The former may be referred to as simply "transphobic," while the latter may be assigned the agreed upon number of pluses.

Troublesome moderates may ask if, rather than figuring out clever ways to ratchet up the intensity of Our language, We ought to tone it down. Maybe, they carp, by broadening the definition of previously exclusive terms like "Nazi," "racist," and "white supremacy," to include things that are systemic, or sometimes just obnoxious, We are watering down the words to the point that eventually no one outside the Woke movement will take them seriously. They point to the rapidly expanding circle of who is racist (see below) as evidence, wondering if perhaps the Woke movement is a self-defeating, contradictory mess that is turning slow progress into possible armed conflict.

Transformation of the word "racism," 2010 to 2020

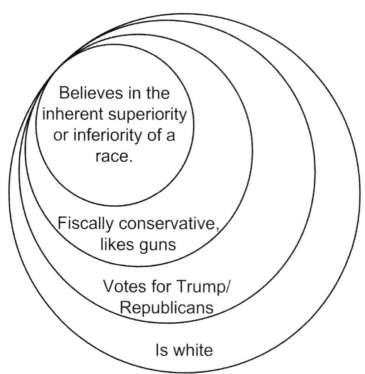

Obviously We need another circle to include people who question the Woke definition of "racist." And if people begin shrugging when We slander them as racist for merely existing, we bump them to "racist+".

Lessons Learned

"I would argue that identity politics is exactly who we are."
— *Stacy Abrams*

Trigger warning: This chapter refers to LatinX people by the outdated, sexist version of the label.

Beyond the honing of tactics, the Woke have nothing left to learn.

Because that is an incredibly arrogant statement, We generally avoid making it. Better to pay lip service to intellectual humility while simultaneously acting with the utmost confidence that We and *only* We have the correct answers to a multitude of devilishly complex problems.

As of this writing, white, heterosexual, cisgendered, Christian, baby boomer male Joe Biden is the President Elect, but President Trump received over 70 million votes. While thoughtful moderates might pause and wonder how someone as intentionally divisive and obviously unfit for the job could have attracted 70 million voters, We know the answer - racism and stupidity.

We are often criticized by moderates for our insight, who say things like:

1. Maybe if you'd stop calling them racist they'd stop voting for people like Trump.
2. Trump attracted nearly 20% of the Black vote, a third of the

Latino[23] vote, and about a quarter of the LGBT-etc vote. They can't all be racist and stupid.

3. Have you sought out an intelligent Trump voter and politely asked them why they're voting for him instead of guessing? As long as you don't insult them they'll probably just tell you.
4. Organizations like BLM were instrumental in turning out Democratic minority voters, but it's impossible to know how many people they mobilized for Trump.

Poppycock.

That Biden barely eked out a victory over the least popular President in modern American history does not indicate We should change, and we reject any self reflection as racism. That the "blue wave" of 2020 House and Senate elections never arrived is not a sign that Americans are just as sick of Our incessant race baiting as they are of President Trump's. If anything, We must double down on the name calling, as most Americans are clearly not getting the message that they are racist and stupid.

And doubling down is precisely what we intend to do. New York Times contributor and economist Robert Reich proposed, in the weeks before the 2020 election, a Truth and Reconciliation committee, which would "name every official, politician, executive, and media mogul whose greed and cowardice enabled this catastrophe." Since the election, many Woke have supported the idea of creating lists of Trump supporters.

Racists across the country denounce the idea of drawing up lists of political opponents for the purpose of punishing them, screeching as if We were opening a Pandora's Box that practically guarantees escalation to the point of violence. Meanwhile, moderates have begun wondering aloud if the Woke making retributive lists means the country is turning a corner, where losing an election may become the life-or-death scenario both tribes have long claimed it to be.

For years, political ads have painted every election as "the most important election ever," attempting to terrify audiences into voting for a specific party by arguing that the other party planned to maliciously target them. It is beyond time to put truth to that previously spurious claim. Any complaints that We will mobilize giant swaths of conservative voters, push

---

23 Please forgive the violent term "Latino." I only include it here to demonstrate moderates' unwillingness to confront the internalized misogyny of their dialect.

horrified moderates toward Republican candidates, or queue Ourselves up for the chopping block when We inevitably lose an election should result in the addition of the concerned speaker's name to one of Our lists.

Some observers wonder if, as President Trump's daily needling of half the country recedes, the Woke will likewise stand down, allowing America to unite behind President-elect Biden and reach compromise solutions that do not alienate giant swaths of otherwise reasonable people. The question is ridiculous. We have not even finished creating an official Enemy List, let alone unleashed the power of the state upon people who disagree with us. Now is not the time for compromise or reason, and the suggestion of either comes from a place of such privilege that it offends Our collective soul.

The overarching lessons of the 2020 elections are:

1. America is virulently racist.
2. The Woke must castigate harder.
3. It is time to punish the intolerant fascists who oppose us.

Bend Every Knee

"I have a plan for that."
— Senator Elizabeth Warren

We have rules for that. It does not matter what the "that" is, We have rules for it. Many rules. Most often these do not *replace* traditional rules, they augment them. Qualitatively, Our rules are superior based on the rapidity of their development and the aggression with which we enforce them.

Traditional rules take decades, often longer, to evolve. While moderates will agree that many took far too long, they lack the spine to slop hundreds of new rules on most daily interactions at Ludicrous Speed. This is where *We* come in.

If you talk, We have rules.
If you date, We have rules.
If you hire someone, We have rules.
If you use emojis, We have rules.
If you debate, or discuss ideas, We have rules.
If you change your hairstyle, We have rules.
If you wear clothing, We have rules.
If you have an opinion, We have rules.
If you consume art, We have rules.
If you *produce* art, We have rules. Oh, so many rules.

As should be clear by now, submission is necessary, but not sufficient. Take the case of white, heterosexual, cisgendered male, and Portland

Mayor Ted Wheeler. Wheeler *thought* he was Woke, because he let nightly riots occur in downtown Portland, chastised President Trump, demanded federal law enforcement officers protecting a federal courthouse leave, and was tear gassed while attending a protest. On the 96th straight night of protests, We arrived at his home to show him he was wrong.

That night, as mostly peaceful protesters outside his home broke windows and lit a fire in the street while shouting for his resignation, Wheeler learned what I asserted in the Introduction - *there is no bar high enough*. Wheeler proved Us right that night by allowing police to break up the "riot" for "safety" reasons.

The moderates who were still paying attention were largely aghast, and murmurs of some secretly considering voting for President Trump in 2020 leaked out. This also proves Our point. Not the point that many moderates who could not stand President Trump suddenly found themselves agreeing with him about civil unrest, the point that moderates are violent racists that must be brought to heel. Fortunately, very few moderates are willing to stand up to Us. By tarring everyone with the "bigot" label, We have focused the hateful energy of a relatively small number of people on one critic at a time, making countless examples of anyone who opposes Our anti-fascist agenda.

Time may not be on Our side, however, as poll after poll shows a majority of Americans scared of speaking their minds on anything, clinging to the racist belief that riots are bad, and generally finding Us as insufferable as President Trump. If We do not accelerate our takeover of mainstream institutions, moderates may continue to route around Us via alternative forms of media, education, and entertainment. They may file lawsuits against employers that force them to sit through creepy re-education sessions that call large swaths of people racist. They may quit those jobs and form competitors that focus on getting their jobs done instead of being Woke. They may flee large city centers where they do not feel safe. They may re-connect with friends of all colors and persuasions, finding commonalities that allow them to enjoy each others' company without Woke intermediaries.

They may gain *class consciousness*, pushing us back to the fringe that our numbers represent, and move forward with actual solutions to America's racial and economic problems.

A terrifying example is Nick Buckley, a white, heterosexual, cisgendered male from Manchester. Buckley was rightly fired in 2020 from the charity he founded and ran for decades, targeting at-risk youth, for posting an article critical of the Black Lives Matter organization. The board of trustees, having received 464 signatures requesting Buckley's termination, complied, only to be sued by Buckley. Buckley was re-instated at his own charity, and the board stepped down.

While this may *seem* like no more than the usual miscarriage of justice one expects from the white patriarchy, it sets the dangerous precedent of due process. Also the fact that the petition to reinstate Buckley garnered over 17,500 signatures may signal to moderates that most people can not stand Us and have noticed that, much like President Trump, We make every bad situation worse.

If these realizations went mainstream it would be a disaster nearly on par with Americans understanding their country within historical or global context. If enough moderates stood their ground against our vacuous accusations, soon everyone would believe it was safe to ignore Us and go about their lives in peace. Worse, Americans focusing on their kinship may make steady progress on the very issues that give Us a reason to avoid getting real jobs. Every time America makes any type of progress it makes the Woke movement less relevant, and more likely We will have to share the country with fascists. We will stop this progress by any means necessary.

Make no mistake about it - the Woke movement is fighting for its life. 2020 America is far too integrated for Us to neatly split into Black vs white. People hear Our message of racial and other strife, then go to work, where they often interact quite pleasantly with coworkers of various skin colors, sexual preferences, or other differences without issue. That gives them eight hours to forget that if they insist on quietly enjoying someone else's company, they must do so under Our guidance.

On our side, We have traditional media outlets choosing overwhelmingly Woke-friendly stories all day, every day. We have sport figures not just quietly taking a knee, but wearing political slogans on clothing, with more slogans painted on courts. We have Human Resource departments across the country frantically developing courses on racial sensitivity. We have social media companies "shadow banning" (a practice where the content remains in place, but is never recommended), or removing unWoke points of view. We have Hollywood enforcing strict racial quotas (Web search: "oscars racial quota"). Even Netflix has Social Justice recommendations, in case their customers were tempted to simply enjoy a movie at the end of a work day.

Finally, we have Covid19, the stealthiest ally the Woke movement has ever harnessed. Physical interactions under Covid19 lockdowns have been replaced by social media interactions, which benefits Us in multiple ways.

1. People are far more inflammatory on social media than in person.
2. One can cultivate which perspectives they hear on social media, ensuring nothing ever contradicts their Truth.
3. We can isolate and mob individuals with nearly programmatic ferocity.

In other words We have a cultural full court press in place, and the more the silent majority wants us to leave them alone, the harder We will press. We will continue to relentlessly badger everyone, reminding them of things they already agree with, like Black lives matter.

If they protest that they are exhausted and just want to eat their dinner, We will scream that people are *dying*.

If they disengage from Us, We will scream that they are *privileged*.

If they push back on anything we believe, We will scream for them to be *cancelled*.

If they listen to conservative points of view, we will scream that they are *alt-right*.

If they have different beliefs than us, We will scream that they are *bigots, or Uncle Toms*.

Some moderates believe that if they give us an inch, we will take a mile. Wrong. *The mile was always ours*. We will never stop screaming. There is no end goal, no finish line. You will never be good enough, and this will never stop. This is your life now.

We will bend every knee.

My Thanks

Thank you for reading this ode to the intellectual disaster that is "White Fragility." If you'd like to see more content like this, please take a moment to leave an honest review on amazon.com. Amazon uses reviews and ratings to know when and how to recommend books.

To be notified of any new books, or receive the occasional short story, please visit https://www.subscribepage.com/tm and sign up for my newsletter. I'll never sell your information or pester you more than about once a month.

Printed in Great Britain
by Amazon